# The Myrour of Recluses

# The Myrour of Recluses

## A Middle English Translation of *Speculum Inclusorum*

Edited by

## Marta Powell Harley

Madison ● Teaneck
Fairleigh Dickinson University Press
London: Associated University Presses

Associated University Presses
440 Forsgate Drive
Cranbury, NJ 08512

Associated University Presses
25 Sicilian Avenue
London WC1A 2QH, England

Associated University Presses
P.O. Box 338, Port Credit
Mississauga, Ontario
Canada L5G 4L8

The paper used in this publication meets the requirements
of the American National Standard for Permanence of Paper
for Printed Library Materials Z39.48-1984.

**Library of Congress Cataloging-in-Publication Data**

Speculum inclusorum. Middle English
   The Myrour of recluses : a Middle English translation of Speculum inclusorum / edited by Marta Powell Harley.
       p.   cm.
   Includes bibliographical references.
   ISBN 0-8386-3589-X (alk. paper)
   1. Hermits—Religious life.   2. Contemplation.   3. Spiritual life—Christianity.   4. Monastic and religious life.   5. Christian literature. Latin (Medieval and modern)—Translations into English (Middle)   6. English language—Middle English, 1100–1500—Texts.
I. Harley, Marta Powell.   II. Title.
BX2845.S6513   1996
255′.02—dc20                                                    95-18178
                                                                     CIP

PRINTED IN THE UNITED STATES OF AMERICA

*for L.A.R. and S.M.S.*

# Contents

# Acknowledgments

I wish to thank the British Library for making available the manuscript of *The Myrour of Recluses;* the Bodleian Library for granting access to Lillian B. Rogers's B. Litt. thesis; Malcolm B. Parkes, Keble College, Oxford, for his generous assistance on paleographical matters; Mirjam Foot, Deputy Director, West European Collections, The British Library, for her expert account of the manuscript binding; Linda E. Voigts, University of Missouri, for useful bibliographical suggestions; and Maureen A. Tilley, Florida State University, for helpful recommendations on medieval Latin.

Grants from the American Philosophical Society in 1983 and Florida State University in 1987 aided my research, and a Florida State University Faculty Sabbatical for 1992–93 enabled me to complete the work.

At the Twenty-Sixth International Congress on Medieval Studies, May 1991, I read an early version of "*The Myrour of Recluses* as Rule, Manual, and Mystical Treatise."

# Introduction

## *THE MYROUR OF RECLUSES*
## AND ITS LATIN SOURCE

The fourteenth-century Latin *Speculum Inclusorum* is preserved in two manuscripts: London, British Library, MS. Royal A.V and Oxford, St. John's College, MS. 177. In 1938 L. Oliger printed in *Lateranum* the Royal A.V version, with corrections from the Oxford manuscript.[1] In his introductory discussion of the date, origin, and authorship of the *Speculum Inclusorum,* Oliger tentatively identified the author, a man of evident ecclesiastical learning, as a Carthusian monk, writing in England at the beginning of the second half of the fourteenth century. Oliger argued that the reference to "episcopi nullatenses" (or "byscopes nullatenses" [61]) suggested a date after Pope Benedict XII (1334–42), who named no titular bishops; from the recommendation that the book be read, if not in Latin, "in English or in French" ("anglico vel gallico"), Oliger inferred a date prior to 1362, the year the English Parliament enacted the Statute of Pleading, mandating the use of English in the courts.[2] Although Oliger may have exaggerated the importance of the Statute of Pleading as a linguistic marker, he found support for his conclusion that England was the physical and spiritual homeland of the *Speculum Inclusorum* in several circumstances: that all manuscripts are English; that, as vernacular alternatives to Latin, English is recommended first and French second; that the terms *servitium debitum* and *servitium divinum* are used instead of the expressions for canonical hours or divine offices; and that the life of the recluse was more in vogue in England than on the Continent.[3]

A Middle English translation of the *Speculum Inclusorum* is preserved in one imperfect, fifteenth-century manuscript, London, British Library, MS. Harley 2372. The only existing edition of the Middle English manuscript is Lillian E. Rogers's unpublished 1933 thesis; however, the Rogers edition was prepared prior to Oliger's

Italian edition of the Latin *Speculum Inclusorum* and without the knowledge of the Latin manuscripts.[4] The title of the present edition, *The Myrour of Recluses,* is editorial. Unaware of the Latin source, Rotha Mary Clay used the title *Book for Recluses* in her 1914 description of the Middle English work,[5] while two decades later Lillian Rogers adopted the title found on the spine of the manuscript's binding, *Advice to Recluses.* In later references to the Middle English text, the title has varied. In his 1955 work *The Religious Orders in England,* David Knowles cited Oliger's *Speculum Inclusarum* [sic] and Rogers's *Advice to Recluses,* apparently not fully aware of their connection.[6] In *A Check-List of Middle English Prose Writings of Spiritual Guidance,* P. S. Jolliffe twice indexed the Middle English work (both times without a title), under "H. Growth in the Spiritual Life" and "O. For Those Living under Rule"; Jolliffe cited Rogers's *Advice to Recluses* and erroneously placed Oliger's publication in *Speculum,* not *Lateranum.*[7] The Middle English work was given the Latin title, *Speculum Inclusorum,* in *A Manual of the Writings in Middle English* and elsewhere.[8] The present title, *The Myrour of Recluses,* borrows the scribe's first spelling of "myro*ur*," found in the final folio. Oliger's suggestion is similar, though he chooses the second of the manuscript's two spellings: "Il titolo della traduzione doveva essere: *Mirror of the Recluses,* nella dizione antica: *Myrrour . . . ,* parola che si riscontra in altra connessione nel testo della traduzione sull'ultimo foglio del codice."[9]

More than two decades ago, Charlotte D'Evelyn observed that "[a] full appraisal of the translator's ability to match the literacy and humane qualities of his Latin original must await the publication of the English text, desirable in spite of its damaged state."[10] By sheer serendipity, the damaged manuscript preserves a text that, though incomplete, is nevertheless coherent. The Latin text consists of a brief prologue and four parts, with each part divided into 3–5 chapters: part 1 includes a preface and four chapters on the motives for embracing the life of the recluse; in three parallel chapters each, parts 2 and 3 examine the nature and pursuit of three aspects of the contemplative life (fervent prayer, devout meditation, and edifying reading); and part 4 concerns the consequent rewards of the vocation. In the Middle English manuscript, part 1 of the treatise is intact, with the exception of the first few lines of the preface (these lines, along with the brief prologue, constitute one lost leaf). From parts 2 and 3, only the third chapters (on edifying reading) are entirely lost. The present edition provides the preface and four chapters of part 1 and the first two chapters of parts 2 and 3 in their entirety, with defects in the Middle English remedied by bracketed Modern English translations of the Latin original (see Appendix A for the Latin passages). Thus, the Middle English *Myrour of Recluses* treats fully the four motives for choosing enclosure and amply examines the nature and practice of prayer and meditation.

## THE TRANSLATION AND ITS AUDIENCE

The Middle English translation found in Harley 2372 follows the division into parts found in the Latin manuscript Royal A.V. The surviving Middle English translation, however, is a copy of a Middle English manuscript, as several scribal errors confirm: for example, a misreading of final, broken-circle *e* produces "hyld" for the more difficult "hyl[e]" (10); the error "deceyuyd" for "dece[rn]yd" shows the misreading of long *r* and *n* (38–39); "dalyaunce" is a scribal misreading of Middle English "Dalida" (362); and "þis *pres*ent lyf" (979–80) must be a mistranscription of English "lyȝt," rather than a mistranslation of Latin "ab hac luce."

The original Middle English translator's overarching aim was to preserve the form and content of his Latin original; as R. Ellis notes, the translator "exercised this choice more often than not,"[11] striving to produce "a translation as close to its original as authorised translations of the Bible were expected to be to theirs."[12] The intention to supply a close and faithful translation is apparent in the treatment of individual words. The translator uses more than two hundred doublets to clarify Latin words. More than half of the doublets are comprised of a form of the Latin word and another Middle English equivalent: for example, "devocione" is translated "deuoc*io*n and almesse" (42), "sustentacio" becomes "sustentac*io*n and beryng vp" (75), and "humilis inclinacio" is expanded to "humble & meke inclinac*io*n or bowynge" (910). In fewer than ten percent of these doublets does the close equivalent of the Latin word come second: "intencio" is translated "sterynge or entenc*io*n" (17–18), "arbitrium" becomes "doom & arbitrement" (304), and "suc-

cursum" produces "relees & socour" (573–74). Slightly fewer than
half of all the doublets in the Middle English translation offer two
words unrelated to the Latin original: for example, "foules and
briddes" (145) translates "avibus"; "songes & karoles" (379) expands "cantica"; and "abreggedist and madist lasse" (1038) translates "minuisti."

Occasionally, the translator glosses a Latin word by supplying a
phrase, introduced with the formula "þat is to seyn." Thus, the
Latin phrase "insensibiles creature" is translated "The insensible
creatures (þat is to seyn, the creatures þat hadde no felynge ne
lyf)" (879–80). Likewise, "prudencia circumspecta" elicits the expanded translation "a circumspect prudence (þat is to seyn, a wys
syȝte, seynge byfore & behynde)" (1151–52). Another example
shows the combination of doublet and explanatory phrase: "nichil
superfluum" is rendered "no superflu or outrageous þinges (þat is
to seyn, ovir-mochil or out of mesure)" (1119–20).

With other additions to the Latin, the translator moves beyond
the conservative aim of verbal clarity. First, as Ellis has noted,
"[w]hen writing for women, translators occasionally gloss the
grammatical and pronominal relations of the original to show readers that they are included."[13] In the Middle English *Myrour of
Recluses*, the term "recluses" is not restricted to men, as we see
in the Middle English addition to the Latin ("prout patet evidencius
de inclusis viventibus sicut debent"): "as yt schewith by euydence
& tokne of recluses (& naamly of anchoresses, þat bien more
streytly closed þan oþir religious men & wommen, enclosed + in
her houses be leue of he[r] souereyns and in alle tymes at her
souereyns wyl)" (394–98). Subsequently, the Middle English feminine form accompanies the masculine, "ancres & ankeresses"
(399), where the Latin masculine plural is understood; and some
lines later, "ancresse" (406) curiously stands alone for "inclusus."
While elsewhere the translator consistently defines his audience
with masculine nouns and pronouns, these occasional changes are
sufficient to widen the audience of a text originally written for
male recluses.

A second effect of additions to the Latin is the easing of some
recommendations. The Latin author's statement, "Non enim ad
statum vestrum pertinet . . . familiam retinere," is qualified by the
Middle English translator, who permits the recluse a maximum of

two servants: "Fforsothe, yt app*er*tenyth nat to youre estat to . . . wiþholde meyne passynge to s*er*uauntȝ" (122–25). In this same passage, the Middle English translator elaborates on the restriction against helping friends and relatives, and again the addition mitigates the rigidity of the Latin original ("Non enim ad statum vestrum pertinet . . . de exhibicione consanguineorum vel amicorum sollicitudinem gerere"):

> Fforsothe, yt app*er*tenyth nat to youre estat . . . to bere the charge of helpynge of ȝoure cosyns and frendes. But ȝif it happe þat a vertuo[u]s p*er*sone, be yt cosyn or ellis, þoruȝ infortune of þe world be driuen to scharp meschief or pouert and hath but smal or no confort of soco*ur* or relief, thanne ys yt good and meritorie to releue suych a p*er*sone. And ȝet, ȝe be more hoolden to releue ȝoure blood, ȝif he be v*er*tuous þan an-oþ*er* strange p*er*sone, ȝouþ it be v*er*tuous & meritorie to releue hem bothe. (122–23, 126–34)

This Middle English continuation, which conceivably could have appeared in an intermediate version, permits the recluse to make a more compassionate response, although the compassion is restricted to virtuous persons, and the recluse's responsibility for relatives is deemed greater than his or her responsibility for friends.

A third impulse, the translator's search for more vivid or concrete expression, explains a handful of the Middle English additions to the Latin. For example, "Ad hoc iudicium" becomes "Vnto þat tre*m*lynge or qu<a>kynge Iugement" (1000), and the Latin phrases "non aperitur" and "pulsanti" are translated metaphorically in "he openeþ nat þe ȝates" (389) and "I knokke at ȝe þate of þi m*er*cy" (1099). In the discussion of the purgation of the Seven Deadly Sins through Christ's physical suffering, the translator makes explicit the connection between Christ's suffering and the individual's avoidance of Envy, drawing graphic meaning from the verb "attenuet" in the Latin clause ("et tuam cupiditatem attenuet Christi nuditas pro te pendentis in cruce"): "and lat þe nakkydnes of Crist hangynge in the croys make þe nakyd and baar*e* of coueytous desir" (920–22).

Reductions of the Latin text are rare. In only a few instances does the Middle English text reduce a Latin doublet to a single word: "ad Dei servicium et honorem" is translated "to Goddys s*er*uise" (236); "aridus et exsiccatus" becomes "drye" (293); and "non desinas, non desistas" is reduced to "stinte nat" (1068). Elements in a series are at times dropped: "vanis, voluptuosis vel inpertinentibus" is reduced to "veyn and inpertynent þinges" (474); "laudem, servicium et honorem" to "seruyse and honour" (731); "excitant, provocant et movent" to "styren an prouoken" (744); and "laudem, gloriam et honorem" to "honoure and worschipe" (768). A longer series—"si quid potencie, si quid prudencie, si quid bonitatis, si quid utilitatis, si quid pulcritudinis, si quid honestatis"—loses two elements in translation: "be yt myȝt, prudence, bountee, or honeste" (817).

While there are inadvertent deletions at lines 795–97 and 913–16 (see the Textual and Explanatory Notes), a deliberate deletion warrants attention. In the Middle English manuscript, the quotation of 1 Cor. 6:10 is curtailed. The Middle English text refers to "a manere [or] spice of 'lecherie agayn kynde,' which is callyd in Latyn of þe apostyl 'molicies'" (412–14); however, the Latin text continues: "ubi dicit quod 'neque molles, neque masculorum concubitores regnum Dei possidebunt.'" The first two categories in 1 Cor. 6:10, "neque molles, neque masculorum concubitores," receive varying translations: the two versions in Forshall and Madden's Wycliffe Bible are "neither neische, neither lecchours of men, that don synne of Sodom" and "nether letchouris aȝen kynde, nether thei that doon letcheri with men,"[14] while the Douay-Rheims translation of the Vulgate has "Nor the effeminate, nor liers with mankind."[15] The deletion in the Middle English is evidently intentional and reflects, not the translator's reticence, but his understanding of a distinction between the two categories offered in the Latin scriptural quotation. As John Boswell observes, "[T]he unanimous tradition of the Church through the Reformation, and of Catholicism well into the twentieth century, has been that the word [*mollitia* or *mollicies*] applied to masturbation."[16] The Middle English translator evidently found the continuation of the scriptural passage superfluous, since the category "masculorum concubitores" is irrelevant to the exemplum of the hermit who heedlessly practiced "þis synne of 'molicies'" (421).

Finally, the Middle English translation identifies no scriptural passages by book and chapter, the general practice in the Latin text. Whether the deletions are the decision of the original translator or a subsequent scribe is, of course, indeterminable.

## *THE MYROUR OF RECLUSES* AS RULE, MANUAL, AND MYSTICAL TREATISE

The place of *The Myrour of Recluses* within the vast body of Middle English religious prose has been variously defined. Its inclusion in Jolliffe's 1974 *Check-List of Middle English Prose Works of Spiritual Guidance* places the work within the broad field of "Middle English prose writings concerned with confession and spiritual guidance,"[17] writings aimed "to instruct and guide Christians as individuals."[18] *The Myrour of Recluses* is among the works in the category "For Those Living under Rule," which includes "tracts written for solitaries as well as those written for members of religious communities."[19] In D'Evelyn's 1970 bibliographical chapter "Instructions for Religious," *The Myrour of Recluses* joins *The Rule of St. Celestine* and *The Rule of St. Linus* in the subcategory "Rules for Hermits and Recluses." According to D'Evelyn, "a rule for recluses tended to become a devotional treatise, a guide for the inner life rather than a series of directions for the outer life."[20] Consistent with this definition is her description of the Latin *Speculum Inclusorum* as "a *borderline* rule more concerned with the inner than with the outer life."[21]

*The Myrour of Recluses* is mentioned in Valerie M. Lagorio's 1981 article on one particularly problematic area in the indexing of religious prose, Middle English mystical prose. Lagorio offers more than a half-dozen subcategories of what she terms the "mystical canon," the body of works "united by its purpose of promoting the attainment of the contemplative life."[22] Lagorio's mystical canon includes four primary categories: (1) "works concerned with the methodology of mysticism" (e.g., *The Cloud of Unknowing* and Walter Hilton's *Scale of Perfection*); (2) "accounts of the unitive experience itself and its significance" (e.g., Julian of Norwich's *Revelations*); (3) "prophetic visions" (e.g., St. Bridget's *Revelations*); and (4) vernacular works of religious instruction written by the mystics themselves (e.g., Richard Rolle's various works).[23] Having suggested that "affective meditations, and especially those on the life and Passion of Christ, be allotted a separate category on the borderline of mystical writing,"[24] Lagorio further enlarges the canon: "Similarly, treatises on the solitary life, such as Aelred of Rievaulx's *De Institutione Inclusarum, Speculum Inclusorum,* the *Ancrene Riwle,* the Bridgettine *Rewyll of Seynt Saviore,* and

Richard Methley's *To Hew Heremyte: A Pystyl of Solytary Lyfe Nowadayes,* should be adjacent to the mystics' writings, since, although these works may emphasize theology and asceticism more than mystical union, the aim of such a solitary vocation was to achieve the *via contemplativa.*"[25]

For D'Evelyn, the relative development of the inner and outer rules in *The Myrour of Recluses* is at issue, but a tripartite distinction is suggested in Lagorio's observation that treatises on the solitary life "may emphasize theology and asceticism more than mystical union." In fact, in the spectrum of adjectives applied to individual works for solitaries, three bands are conspicuous: "ascetic" and "penitential," "devotional" and "theological," "contemplative" and "mystical." Lagorio contends that the *Speculum Inclusorum* is more ascetic and theological than it is mystical or contemplative, and she sandwiches the title between two works that are inarguably more ascetic than mystical. The grouping is unsatisfactory. Indeed, Ann K. Warren has observed that the *Ancrene Riwle* and Aelred's *De Institutione Inclusarum,* on the one hand, and such works as the *Speculum Inclusorum,* on the other, exemplify the mid-fourteenth-century "shift of emphasis" from the anchorite as "a penitential ascetic" to the anchorite as "a contemplative":

> Extant anchorite literature up to the mid-fourteenth century is ascetic in thrust and skirts mystical themes even though anchorites represent a class of religious whose sole raison d'etre is 'contemplative.' . . . Thus, although the purpose of all anchorite rules is to aid, supposedly, in the transformation of self that alone, with God's grace, will take one up the ladder that reaches to Him, the documents written in the earlier centuries rarely even approach the ascent of that ladder. . . . When, in such works as Goscelin's *Liber confortatorius,* Aelred's *De institutis inclusarum* and the *Ancrene Riwle* . . . , the achievement of the mystical moment is mentioned, it is noted only casually in passing. . . . In marked contrast to this, the literature of the second-half of the fourteenth century, most notably Rolle's work and Hilton's *Scale of Perfection,* but including also the anonymous *Speculum inclusorum,* leads the anchorite toward mystical union with God in explicit and joyous terms. Here the purgative way is clearly only a beginning, purification a first step. The goal of the contemplative life is stated and embraced. It is a goal to be achieved.[26]

To better understand and describe *The Myrour of Recluses* as a work on the solitary life, we may assess the relative weight of *The Myrour*'s outer rule (its ascetic directives on the physical life) and its inner rule (its teachings on theology and the contemplative life). *The Myrour of Recluses* serves reasonably well as an outer rule. The author provides practical advice on choosing enclosure and outlines the primary regulations governing the solitary's physical life. In part 1, chapter 1, recluses are warned against embracing the enclosed life with such misguided intentions as enjoying greater rest or freedom, securing better support for family and friends, or acquiring more worldly goods. In part 1, chapter 2, the author unfolds a sound method for assuming the solitary life: the prospective recluse must choose two or three mentors to oversee a year-long apprenticeship, during which time the individual is to live even more strictly than recluses do; at the conclusion of the year, having prayed for guidance and having received the assent of the appointed advisers, the prospective recluse may make a vow, a vow that "schal be kept vnto þe end[e], o[n] peyne of eternel and euere-lastinge dampnacion" (224–26).

*The Myrour of Recluses* contains the customary regulations on clothing and diet. Recluses are urged to choose "symple cloþinge" (137), eschewing "gay and precious cloþinges" (93–94); the author, in fact, subsequently associates such "gay & neyce aparail and clopi[s]" (108–9) with the men and women commonly visiting the reprehensibly worldly recluses of the cities. Recluses must also avoid "delycat metys and drynkes" (94), contenting themselves with "mene foode and sustenaunce" (137); however, echoing Richard Rolle's warning in *The Form of Living*—"Some er begylde with ovre mikell abstinens of mete and drynk and slepe, þat es of þe temptacion of þe devell"[27]—the author of *The Myrour of Recluses* warns recluses against allowing the Fiend to tempt them into immoderate self-discipline: "More-ovir, I desire þat ȝe wacche bisili agayn þe temptacions of þe feend, þat noþing sleuthe or lache ouyr-mochil þe stiburn hardnesse of ȝoure lyf vndir colour of fals necessite, ne noþing augmente or ecche it ouyr ȝour force or myȝt, but aftir þe doom & arbitrement of discrecion, chastise & nursche ȝoure body in diuerse tymes, þat it be soget on þat o side to þe commaundement of ȝoure spirites & suffisaunt on þat oþir part to performe & fulfille þe labour enioyned to þe body" (300–8).

Speech and social contact are strictly circumscribed. Solitaries

must abstain from "vnhonest, unprofitable, and ydil talkyng*es*"
(97). If visitors are permitted to recount "tydyng*es* & auentures
þ*at* fallen in diu*er*se contrees" (110–11), recluses will find their
imaginations vexed thereafter with "diu*er*se fantasies" (115). Recluses are not to maintain a household of more than two servants,
nor are their dwellings to serve as schools for "ʒoong folk" (125)
or as inns for pilgrims or relatives, although helping the virtuous
poor is not strictly forbidden.[28] Recluses are to please God by
persevering in good works.

   *The Myrour of Recluses* gives greater attention to the inner rule.
While the elements of the outer rule are certainly intended to foster
an increasingly satisfying spirituality, the inner rule expressly gov-
erns the recluse's devotional and contemplative pursuits. *The Myrour of Recluses* draws throughout on devotional and doctrinal
material familiar to the general audiences of the popular religious
manuals. Scores of manuals or handbooks of religious instruction
survive from the Middle Ages. Their growth over a three-hundred-
year period is largely attributable to Innocent III's Fourth Lateran
Council in 1215, which made annual confession obligatory, and to
Archbishop Pecham's Council of Lambeth in 1281, which prescribed the fundamental topics for religious instruction. Among
the topics prescribed in chapter 9 of the canons of the Council of
Lambeth are the Articles of the Faith, the Ten Commandments,
the Seven Works of Mercy, the Seven Deadly Sins, the Seven
Principal Virtues, and the Seven Sacraments. With time, the contents of the religious manuals expanded to include such popular
topics as the Five Bodily Wits, the Five Ghostly Wits, the Seven
Gifts of the Holy Ghost, the Pater Noster, Ave Maria, and Creed.
Just as the contents of individual manuals varied, the treatment of
each topic might range from a brief outline to a full discussion; the
manual might be in Latin or the vernacular, and its individual
works might appear in either verse or prose. The audience for the
religious manual was broad, since the prescriptions of the Council
of Lambeth were aimed at educating priests and laity alike.[29]

   *The Myrour of Recluses* is not an anthology of instructive texts,
nor is its aim confined to preparing individual Christians for effective confession, but elements of the popular religious manual are
conspicuous in the work, a fact that suggests a potentially wider
audience than the prospective or confirmed recluse. From the preface of part 1 to the final chapter of part 3, more than a half-dozen

rudimentary topics of religious instruction are raised in *The Myrour of Recluses*. For example, in the final chapter, the author recalls the Articles of the Faith in his warning against excessive reliance on human reason: "But for the error þat may be of vndirstondynge, it profite[t]h þat þe Articles of þe Feyth, þat ben conteyned in the Byleve of þe Apostles and in þe Byleve of Athanasie, be fully vndirstonden, bele[eu]ed stedefastly, and taken vn-to memorie or mynde" (1205–9). Sacramental teaching on the eucharist follows (1218–80). Preparatory to the discussion of the efficacy of prayer is a clear statement on the virtue of the Pater Noster: "For þe Dominical preiere (þat is to seyn, þe *Pater Noster*) ys nat so ordeyned ne maad of God þat we scholde al-oonly vse þo wordes in oure preiere, but þat we schul aske non oþir þing in oure preieres þat is sentencialy conteynyd in þat saame. And, forsoþe, it contenyth & comprehendiþ al þat is necessarie to helþe of mannes soule & of his body" (635–41).

The Five Bodily Wits are used prominently. The Five Bodily Wits supply the organizing principle for the third chapter of part 1: "The fyve wyttis of þe body as vn-wys messageres of mannes herte ben accustumed and wont alwey & ouyral to recorde in hemself al þat þei han take and receyuyd, be yt veyn þinges, or vnprofitable, anoyinge, greuynge, or enclynynge vn-to synne" (341–45). Though the teaching in the chapter is general, in a few passages the narrower audience of the recluse is apparent. Following a catalogue of verbal sins, the author imagines the quietness of the recluse's world: "O blessyd is þe ere þat ys so prudently disposid þat he openeþ nat þe ʒates agayn suych vnleefful noyses; & ys schyt & spered agayn þe voluptuous or lusty melodyes of the world; & ys stoppyd agayn alle þo sounes of temptacions, but in-as-mochel as ys possible to hym þat lyueth in þis valeye of wrecchidnesse; & kepith h[y]m a-feer from alle worldly vanytes, as yt schewith by euydence & tokne of recluses (& naamly of anchoresses, þat bien more streytly closed þan oþir religious men & wommen, enclosed + in her houses be leue of he[r] souereyns and in alle tymes at her souereyns wyl)" (388–98). Similarly, in the admonitions against inordinate touching, the exemplum of the ravished hermit is especially applicable to the life of the recluse. Closing the discussion of sight, hearing, touching, smelling, and tasting, the author observes that "Suich contynuel occasions of synnes, þat comen of þe fyve wyttes in a seculer lyf, many of oure olde fadres were wont to fle & eschewe; þerfor, þei desired & coueytid to be closyd in a streyt place where-as they myȝten haue oon necessarie foode and cloþinge" (441–45). The Five Wits are used later in a striking example of the affective meditation: we are asked to apprehend, through our own five senses, Christ's graphically described suffering in the Five Wits—suffering that pardoned our sinful five senses (850–78).

Following a spare reference to the Seven Works of Mercy, the Seven Deadly Sins receive significant attention. As with the Five Wits, the Seven Sins are incorporated into an affective meditation on the Passion: Pride, Envy, Covetousness, and Wrath are sequentially purged by the blood from Christ's head, heart, hands, and body; Christ's bloody sweat and his hunger, fasting, and thirst, "which weryn fillid by þe bittyrnesse of eysil and gall" (934–35), destroy Gluttony; the blood of his circumcision conquers Lust; and the blood from his feet curbs Sloth. Of the Seven Deadly Sins, Sloth seems of greatest consequence to the author. Not only is it given the emphatic final position in the passage outlined above, but it frequently occurs in incidental references. Sloth is paired with Wrath in the reference to "wrathful and sleuthi folk" (25–26) and in the admonition "let n[e] ire disturble or lette ȝow fro the contynuance of vertuous werkes, ne slouþe tarie ȝow þat vnmesurably ys accus[tu]med and wont to tempte ydyl folk" (140–42). Elsewhere, Sloth's kinship with Lust is evident in the phrases "voluptuus sleuthe or sleuthi fleschly lust" (48) and in the assurance that "glotonye" provokes "dulnesse & sleuthe" (438–39).

The preoccupation with Sloth is consistent with three effective rhetorical devices in the work: the depiction of the Christian afterlife, the metaphor of spiritual knighthood, and the hortatory use of 1 Corinthians 1:26. As protection against "presumpcion, negligence, or slouthe" (987–88), the author provides a staple of religious manuals, a harrowing vision of judgment and punishment; the account in part 2, chapter 2 (988–1038), is a development of the references in part 1, chapter 2 (317–28), where allusions to the inexpressible pains of purgatory and hell accompany an endorsement of charitable works and prayers for the souls in purgatory. Implicit criticism of Sloth is found in the numerous references to fighting against temptations (or against the fiend); the calls to combat generally recall 2 Tim. 4:7, while the mention of the crown of victory (430–32) owes a debt to verse 8 in the passage: "I have fought a good fight, I have finished my course, I have kept the faith. As to the rest, there is laid up for me a crown of justice, which the Lord the just judge will render to me in that day" (Douay-Rheims Version). The metaphor of the Christian—or here, more specifically, the recluse—as Christ's knight is introduced at line 118 in an apostrophe, "O gentil knyʒtes of Ihesu Crist"; the later allusion to "Cristes knyth" (432) relies more closely on 2 Tim. 2:3: "Labour as a good soldier of Christ Jesus." The phrase "spirituel bataylle" (430–31, 1109) and the injunction "takeþ agayn þe armes of spiritual knyʒthode" (312–13) look back to 2 Cor. 10:3–4: "For though we walk in the flesh, we do not war according to the flesh. For the weapons of our warfare are not carnal" (Douay-Rheims Version). The allusion to "þe armes" is but a faint echo of the allegory of Christian armor found in Eph. 6:10–17, an allegory that "developed into a literary *topos* of widespread application in the Middle Ages."[30]

Though perhaps less directly than the reminders of purgatorial punishments and the calls to spiritual battle, the quotation of 1 Cor. 1:26 at the very end of each chapter urges a vigilance and commitment wholly alien to the slothful, whom Langland personified so well in his bleary-eyed, somnolent Sloth. The force of the command, "byholdeþ & seeþ ʒoure callynge" (559), is augmented not only through its repetition, but through the author's use of other scriptural passages that encourage a similar watchfulness: "Taak heede & seeth" (455–56; Ps. 45:11); "Seeth þe werkes of God" (828; Ps. 65:5); "Seeth þe Kyng Salomon" (1057; Song of Sol. 3:11); "Taketh hede . . . and seeth" (892; Lam. 1:12); "Seeth, waketh, and preyeth" (610; Mark 13:33); and "Seeth and beholdiþ ʒoure owen self" (121; 2 John 1:8). Persistently enjoining the readers to *see* themselves and others, the author of *The Myrour of Recluses* heightens the significance of the title of his work; the book itself is a mirror reflecting the requirements of the vocation, and in this mirror the prospective recluses must measure their spiritual fitness and ultimately find their own reflections.

The reliance on the popular catechetical topics of the religious handbook is in accord with other works addressed to recluses. In "Varieties of Middle English Religious Prose," Norman F. Blake acknowledges this phenomenon in his category "Rules for conduct for a particular way of life": "The difficulty in allocating texts to this group is that although some were written for specialized audiences, they were often read more widely as texts of general applicability."[31] For example, the five senses are the focus of the second book of the *Ancrene Riwle,* and M. B. Salu has commented on the generic applicability of the *Ancrene Riwle's* treatment of confession: "It is not, I think, difficult to see the reflection of all this [i.e., the production of manuals for confessors] in the sections on Confession and Temptation in the *Ancrene Riwle,* and particularly to see the influence of the manuals. . . . Whether or not exact sources for the *Ancrene Riwle* in this particular are ever discovered, there can be no doubt, to my mind, that the author was in touch with the development in theology which these manuals represent, and indeed his chapter on confession might be taken as itself making a contribution to this particular type of literature."[32] In Edmund Rich's *Speculum Ecclesiae,* a mid-thirteenth-century work written in French and later translated into Latin and English, one section could easily stand alone as a religious manual: an explanation of the usefulness of Holy Scripture in contemplation leads to the treatment of such standard topics as the Seven Deadly Sins, the Ten Commandments, the Articles of the Faith, the Seven Sacraments, the Seven Gifts of the Holy Ghost, and the joys of heaven and pains of hell.[33] In his "Form of Living," Rolle provides four topics profitably kept in mind (the brevity of life, the unpredictability of the time of death, the certainty of judgment, the joys of heaven and the pains of hell), outlines the sins of "hert, and mouth, and dede,"[34] and reviews the three steps of penance—contrition, confession, and satisfaction. Likewise, *The Cloud of Unknowing* reviews the Seven Deadly Sins,[35] while in Hilton's *Scale of Perfection* meditation on the state of the soul invites consideration of the Seven Deadly Sins and the Five Wits.[36] Blake, in fact, observes that "Hilton's *Scala Perfectionis* was written for a recluse but contained much that was of a broader application."[37] Similarly, in "The Audience for the Middle English Mystics," S. S. Hussey calls attention to "chapters of the first book [of Hilton's *Scale*] which, if excerpted, could stand simply as fundamental Christian teaching for all classes of men and women."[38]

While *The Myrour's* incorporation of material from religious manuals is extensive, the ultimate aim of *The Myrour's* inner rule is to further the practice of contemplation. The second part (or last two-thirds) of *The Myrour of Recluses* (452–1280) turns from concerns about the recluse's physical life to a full engagement with the spiritual life. The practice of contemplation is central: "ʒe recluses schul byholde and seen in þis caas and haue good consideracion wher-to ʒe ben principaly callyd & clept, for ʒe ben callyd to þe exercise or vsage [of] contemplatyf lyf" (560–63). The transition cannot surprise us, for in the preface to part 1, we learn that the fourth chapter will address the loftiest motivation for becoming a recluse—the intention to attend "the more frely to dyuyn contemplacion" (22–23). In that fourth chapter, the author defines the three practices essential to contemplation—"preyere, meditacion, & redynge" (471)—and urges the withdrawal of the heart, wit, and body from worldly things, which greatly hinder the three pursuits. The discussion of prayer in *The Myrour of Recluses* is contained in the first chapters of parts 2 and 3, the discussion of meditation in the second chapters of parts 2 and 3. *The Myrour of Recluses* does not formalize prayer into categories, but the author prescribes meditation on "foure þinges" (749)—God's power, his wisdom or truth, his mercy or charity, and his righteousness. The first two elements are subsumed in a meditation on the Creation, with the Passion and Judgment serving as topics of meditation exemplifying God's love and righteousness. Through meditation, the solitary is able "to ascende and clymbe to þe heyest degre of perfeccion" (192–93).

The loss of the third chapters of parts 2 and 3 in *The Myrour of Recluses* eliminates reading from a full consideration. The order of the three pursuits in *The Myrour of Recluses* actually inverts the customary order. For example, in Hilton's *Scale of Perfection* and the anonymous *Cloud of Unknowing,* the order is reading, meditation, and prayer, and the twelfth-century *Scala Claustralium* of Guigo II follows the same order for the first three of its four rungs: "Put simply, the exercise consists of a reading of scripture, reasoned meditation upon its hidden truth, a turning to God in fervent prayer, and a lifting of the mind to God through contemplation."[39] *The Myrour*'s coincidental loss of the sections on reading happens to correspond to the relative treatment of the three practices in other contemplative works. The author of *The Cloud of Unknowing* prescribes "menes . . . in þe whiche a contemplatiif prentys schuld be ocupyed, þe whiche ben þeese: Lesson, Meditacion, & Oryson. Or elles to þin vnderstondyng þei mowe be clepid: Redyng, þinkyng & Preiing."[40] However, while the author of *The*

*Cloud* comments further on meditation and prayer in the four following chapters, he nevertheless neglects reading. Similarly, Walter Hilton introduces the "three means most commonly employed by those who devote themselves to contemplation; these are reading the Holy Scriptures and books of spiritual guidance, meditation, and constant prayer. Since you are not able to read the Holy Scriptures, you should spend more time in prayer and meditation."[41] Respecting this deficiency in his audience, Hilton neglects reading, while focusing chapters 24–33 of book one on prayer and chapters 34–40 on meditation. Indeed, reading is later replaced by a more general recommendation: "So whatever form of prayer, meditation, or activity leads you to the highest and purest desire for Him, and to the deepest experience of Him, will be the means by which you may best seek and find Him."[42]

In sum, the Middle English *Myrour of Recluses* serves adequately as an outer rule, covering those practical and physical aspects of the life that would have been visible to mentors, as well as to visitors to the recluse's window. Complementing the ascetic aims of the outer rule, the inner rule contains much standard devotional and doctrinal teaching, along with plentiful quotations from the scriptures (see Appendix B). The ascetic advice and devotional instruction in *The Myrour of Recluses* serve the higher aim of contemplation. The author's desire to secure for recluses "so mochel swetnesse of þe love of God & of contemplacion þat thei sauoure nat in erþely þinges" (187–89) echoes not only Rolle's sensuous language, but also his announced focus in the second half of *The Form of Living* on "luf" and "contemplatyf lyfe."[43] Only the fragmentary status of *The Myrour of Recluses* diminishes its status as a mystical or contemplative work, for in the *Speculum Inclusorum,* part 4 unfolds the rewards of contemplation in this life and the hereafter. As the author assures the prospective recluses at the beginning of part 3, chapter 2 (the last chapter surviving in *The Myrour of Recluses*), "true meditation advances when it . . . fixes the mind on heavenly things. . . . In meditations of this kind, many have advanced, because many have some foretaste of the sweetness of future blessedness in the delectation of divine goodness and his high beauty, in the revelation of future things, in the conversation of the angels, but also in some sort of vision and ineffable consolation of the Almighty Himself."

## THE MANUSCRIPT

British Library, MS. Harley 2372 is a leather-bound manuscript of 38 parchment leaves, with four paper flyleaves (two front and two back). The binding is of brown calf with gold-tooled fillets and a blind-tooled roll; the label on the spine, "Advice to Recluses," is contemporary with the binding.[44]

The unnumbered parchment leaf at the beginning of the manuscript bears on the recto a recipe for gout and on the verso a note on ownership; this leaf is not part of a larger gathering. The Middle English *Myrour of Recluses,* occupying the thirty-seven numbered folios, consists of five gatherings of eight: $1^8$ (wants i and ii), fols. 1–6; $2^8$, fols. 7–14; $3^8$, fols. 15–22; $4^8$, fols. 23–30; $5^8$ (wants iv), fols. 31–37. Gatherings four and five are discontinuous. Catchwords are found on folios 6v ("in þat"), 14v ("sythe in"), 22v ("-rie for"), and 30v ("of hem"); catchwords on folio 37v are lost due to damage to the bottom of the leaf.

The leaves measure 224 x 150 mm, with a writing space of 146 x 90 mm. There are twenty-three ruled lines of text per page (excepting fol. 37v, where one and a half lines are added). The ink is brown. A four-line lluminated initial ("T") is found on fol. 13v; three-line illuminated initials ("S" and "ȝ") appear on fols. 17r and 22r. The headnotes "Prima," "Secunda," and "Tercia" on the verso and "pars" on the recto are in red ink; fol. 6v erringly bears "pars," and fols. 16v and 17r bear "Prima pars" and "Secunda pars," respectively. Red and blue capitula alternate throughout, while numerous capital letters and, occasionally, the extended ascenders of letters on the top line are highlighted in yellow. Marginalia include a few pointing fingers, frequent use of "nota," and occasional phrases, several in a later hand (transcribed in the Textual and Explanatory Notes following the text).

The script is a hybrid (or bastard) secretary with some anglicana forms; although the letters are formed currently, the proportions are those of textura. Among the scribe's distinctive secretary graphs are single-lobed *a,* the short *r,* and final two-compartment *s.* The secretary *g* is used occasionally, but the two-compartment *g* predominates; the hand contains anglicana graphs, such as the long *r,* and very rarely the double-lobed *a,* although the sigma *s* of anglicana is not found. The *w* is a variant of anglicana. The relative proportions of the ingredients in this mixed hand suggest a date in the mid-fifteenth century.[45]

MS. Harley 2372 appears as item 9430 in Angus McIntosh, M. L. Samuels, and Michael Benskin's *Linguistic Atlas of Late Medieval English*. Based on the manuscript's "Linguistic Profile,"[46] the dialect of the manuscript is placed at coordinates 530 and 209 on the dialect map,[47] a point in southeastern Hertfordshire between Hertford and St. Albans.

The note on the verso of the manuscript's first parchment leaf reads, "Thys ys a good bok ffor holy men or wemen, the whyche bok bylongeth to the almes-howse off Wyll*i*am Brown in Stawnford in the dyocesse off Lyncoln, by the gyft off S*ir* John Trvs, chapleyn to the seyd Wyll*i*am Brown su*m*-tyme and prest in the seyd beyd-howse. Orate, q*ue*so, legentes, p*ro* a*n*i*m*a dicti D*om*i*ni Ioha*nn*is."

References to the foundation of William Brown's almshouse are numerous. In the Patent Rolls, the earliest mention is a 1485 entry:

> Licence for William Broun of Staumford, co. Lincoln, one of the merchants of the staple of Calais, who has newly built a chapel and divers other houses and buildings within the town of Staumford for an almshouse, to found an almshouse at Staumford of a warden and a brother, both secular chaplains, to pray for the good estate of the king and his consort Anne, queen of England, and the said William and Margaret his wife and for their souls after death, to be called the almshouse of William Broun.[48]

Eight years later, a 1493 entry in the Patent Rolls sheds further light on the foundation:

> Whereas William Browne of Staunford, co. Lincoln, one of the staple of Calais, had proposed to build a chapel and houses in the town of Staunford for divers chaplains and poor of both sexes for an almshouse, but was prevented by death; license for Thomas Stokke, clerk, the brother of Dame Margaret Browne, relict of the said William Browne, and executrix of the will of the said William, to found an almshouse at Staumford aforesaid, of one warden and one brother, both being secular chaplains, to celebrate divine service for the good estate of the king, Elizabeth the Queen, Reynold Bray, knight, Catherine his wife, the said Thomas Stokke, Elizabeth Elmes and William Elmes, and for their souls after death, and for the souls of William Browne and Margaret his wife, to be called William Browne's almshouse in Staunford; and

license for them to acquire in mortmain lands and rents . . . for the support of these and divers poor of both sexes there according to the ordinance of the said Thomas.[49]

Royal sanction is granted with the 5 February 1494 entry in the Patent Rolls: "License, in pursuance of a license of 28 November last, for Thomas Stokke or his executors to make an almshouse accordingly of a capital messuage in Staunford, with a chapel and other premises for a warden and brother, both secular chaplains." As Rogers reported, the original written accounts of the almshouse for the years 1495–1518 survive in Bodleian Library MS. Rawlinson B.352. The almshouse, or hospital, earned the following description in *The Itinerary of John Leland, in or about the Years 1535–43:* "In the southe parte of Staunford tounne withyn the waulles and by the market place is an hospitale *omnium Sanctorum,* founded by one Broune of that toune, a marchant of a very wonderful richenesse, and he lyvid *in hac aetate.* So that sum men be alyve that have seene hym."[50]

No other contemporary references to John Trus, the manuscript's donor, have been recovered.[51] In the notice on the flyleaf of Harley 2372, the word "su*m*-tyme" may imply that, at the time John Trus donated the manuscript to the almshouse, William Brown had already died. We know from an entry in the Patent Rolls concerning a manorial grant, that by 10 November 1489 both William Brown and his wife Margaret had died. John Trus himself may have died by 1494, since his name does not appear in the 1495–1518 records of almshouse appointments. Thus, the manuscript was perhaps contributed to William Brown's almshouse between 1489 and 1495. The manuscript came to the British Museum with the acquisition of the Harleian manuscripts in the mid-eighteenth century.

## EDITORIAL METHOD

The edited text preserves the spelling of the Middle English manuscript, including *þ, ʒ, ff,* and tailed *i* (printed as *j*). The letters *u* and *v,* as well as the *w* written *vv,* are unaltered. Punctuation and capitalization are modernized. Letters supplied in the expansion of contractions and suspensions are italicized in the edited text and conform to the predominant spelling elsewhere in the manuscript. The flourish or tilde of final *n* is treated as otiose; the bar through *h* and *l* (or *ll*) is disregarded, unless clearly indicating a suspension; and recurved final long-*r* is expanded "-*re*." The ampersand is recorded as such. Supralinear letters, except in abbreviations of numbers, are printed on line.

Where the manuscript separates words now commonly written as one, I join them with a hyphen; falsely joined words are silently separated. Emendations are always indicated: square brackets enclose substitutions or additions of letters or words; diamond brackets surround illegible or partially effaced letters; and a supralinear plus sign signals an editorial omission from the manuscript. Where possible, editorial substitutions or additions conform to the spelling of the manuscript.

Bracketed Modern English translations of the Latin original are supplied to complete fragmentary chapters in the manuscript; the Latin passages are found in Appendix A. The titles of parts and chapters are editorial, as are the bracketed identifications of scriptural quotations; the scriptural citations are indexed in part 1 of Appendix B, while in part 2, for the benefit of scholars interested in late medieval biblical translation, the scriptural translations of the Middle English text are juxtaposed to the Wycliffe translations. Appendix C supplies an Index of Names. Glosses for difficult or unusual Middle English words and phrases are among the entries in the Textual and Explanatory Notes following the edited text.

# NOTES

1. Livarius Oliger, "Speculum Inclusorum," *Lateranum*, n.s., 4 (1938): 1–148.
2. Ibid., 36–40.
3. Ibid., 40–45.
4. Lillian E. Rogers, "Edition of British Museum MS. Harley 2372 (Advice to Recluses)" (B. Litt. thesis, Oxford University, 1933).
5. Rotha Mary Clay, *The Hermits and Anchorites of England* (1914; reprint, Detroit: Singing Tree Press, 1968), 99.
6. David Knowles, *The Religious Orders in England, Volume II: The End of the Middle Ages* (Cambridge: Cambridge University Press, 1955), 121 n. 3.
7. P. S. Jolliffe, *A Check-List of Middle English Prose Writings of Spiritual Guidance* (Toronto: Pontifical Institute of Mediaeval Studies, 1974), no. 28 on 102, no. 40 on 145.
8. Charlotte D'Evelyn, "Instructions for Religious," in *A Manual of the Writings in Middle English, II,* ed. J. Burke Severs (Hamden: Connecticut Academy

of Arts and Sciences, 1970), 480; Valerie M. Lagorio, "Problems in Middle English Mystical Prose," in *Middle English Prose: Essays on Bibliographical Problems,* ed. A. S. G. Edwards and Derek Pearsall (New York: Garland, 1981), 136; Ann K. Warren, "Old Forms with New Meanings: Changing Perceptions of Medieval English Anchorites," *Fifteenth-Century Studies* 5 (1982): 211.

9. Oliger, "Speculum Inclusorum," 28.

10. D'Evelyn, "Instructions," 480.

11. R. Ellis, "The Choices of the Translator in the Late Middle English Period," in *The Medieval Mystical Tradition in England: Papers Read at Dartington Hall, July 1982,* ed. Marion Glasscoe (Exeter: University of Exeter, 1982), 24.

12. Ibid., 25.

13. Ibid., 27–28.

14. *The Holy Bible Made from the Latin Vulgate by John Wycliffe and His Followers,* ed. Josiah Forshall and Frederic Madden (1850; reprint, New York: AMS Press, 1982).

15. *The Holy Bible Translated from the Latin Vulgate: Douay-Rheims Version,* ed. Bishop Richard Challoner (1749–52; reprint, Rockford, IL: TAN Books, 1989).

16. John Boswell, *Christianity, Social Tolerance, and Homosexuality: Gay People in Western Europe from the Beginning of the Christian Era to the Fourteenth Century* (Chicago: University of Chicago Press, 1980), 107.

17. Jolliffe, *Check-List,* 23.

18. Ibid., 28.

19. Ibid., 54. For "a brief survey of what is known about medieval anchorites and their background," see Robert W. Ackerman and Roger Dahood, eds. and trans., *Ancrene Riwle: Introduction and Part I,* Medieval and Renaissance Texts and Studies, no. 31 (Binghamton, NY: Center for Medieval and Early Renaissance Studies, 1984), 7–16.

20. D'Evelyn, "Instructions," 478.

21. Ibid., 480 (my emphasis).

22. Lagorio, "Problems," 136.

23. Ibid., 133.

24. Ibid., 135.

25. Ibid.

26. Warren, "Old Forms," 209–11.

27. Richard Rolle, "The Form of Living," in *English Writings of Richard Rolle, Hermit of Hampole,* ed. Hope Emily Allen, (1931; reprint, Gloucester, Eng.: Sutton, 1988), 86.61–63.

28. For similar advice on social contact and household management, see Aelred of Rievaulx, *Aelred of Rievaulx's "De Institutione Inclusarum": Two English Versions,* eds. John Ayto and Alexandra Barratt, Early English Text Society, o.s., 287 (New York: Oxford University Press, 1984), 1.26–36, 2.39–42, 3.92–118, and 4.153–55.

29. See Marta Powell Harley, "A Fifteenth-Century Manual of Religious Instruction in Bodleian Library MS. Tanner 201," *Fifteenth-Century Studies* 15 (1989): 147.

30. Michael Evans, "An Illustrated Fragment of Peraldus's *Summa* of Vice: Harleian MS 3244," *Journal of the Warburg and Courtauld Institutes* 45 (1982): 17. For a summary of Middle English devotional works that employ the metaphor of spiritual armor, see Evans, 30.

31. Norman F. Blake, "Varieties of Middle English Religious Prose," in *Chaucer and Middle English Studies in Honour of Rossell Hope Robbins,* ed. Beryl Rowland (London: George Allen & Unwin, 1974), 350.

32. M. B. Salu, trans., *The Ancrene Riwle (The Corpus MS.: Ancrene Wisse)* (Notre Dame, IN: University of Notre Dame Press, 1956), xx–xxi.

33. Eric Colledge, ed., *The Mediaeval Mystics of England* (New York: Charles Scribner's Sons, 1961), 50–53, 132.

34. Rolle, "Form of Living," 97.8–9.

35. Phyllis Hodgson, *"The Cloud of Unknowing" and Related Treatises,* Analecta Cartusiana, no. 3 (Salzburg: Institut für Anglistik und Amerikanistik, 1982), 20.13–36.

36. Walter Hilton, *The Ladder of Perfection,* trans. Leo Sherley-Price (1957; reprint, New York: Penguin, 1988), bk. 1, chaps. 52–76, pp. 63–95, and bk. 1, chaps. 78–82, pp. 96–100.

37. Blake, "Varieties," 350.

38. S. S. Hussey, "The Audience for the Middle English Mystics," in *De Cella in Seculum: Religious and Secular Life and Devotion in Late Medieval England,* ed. Michael G. Sargent (Cambridge, Eng.: D. S. Brewer, 1989), 113. For further discussion, see Joseph E. Milosh, *"The Scale of Perfection" and the Religious-Handbook Tradition,* in *"The Scale of Perfection" and the English Mystical Tradition* (Madison: University of Wisconsin Press, 1966), 140–68.

39. George R. Keiser, "'Noght how lang man lifs; bot how wele': The Laity and the Ladder of Perfection," in *De Cella in Seculum: Religious and Secular Life and Devotion in Late Medieval England,* ed. Michael G. Sargent (Cambridge, Eng.: D. S. Brewer, 1989), 147.

40. Hodgson, *Cloud,* 39.23–26.

41. Hilton, *Ladder,* bk. 1, chap. 15, p. 15.

42. Ibid., bk. 1, chap. 46, p. 57.

43. Rolle, "Form of Living," 103.215–16.

44. According to Mirjam Foot, Deputy Director of West European Collections at the British Library (pers. com. 1990), the roll belonged to Christopher Chapman, one of Lord Harley's binders mentioned frequently in Cyril Ernest Wright and Ruth C. Wright, eds., *The Diary of Humfrey Wanley, 1715–1726,* 2 vols. (London: Bibliographical Society, 1966). As Foot notes, Wanley does not mention the manuscript in his diary, presumably because it is not one of the grander bindings. Foot suggests that Wanley may have specified the title "Advice to Recluses."

45. Malcolm B. Parkes (pers. com. 1990) generously contributed his expertise to the description and dating of the hand.

46. Angus McIntosh, M. L. Samuels, and Michael Benskin, *A Linguistic Atlas of Late Medieval English,* 4 vols. (Aberdeen: Aberdeen University Press, 1986), 3:181.

47. Ibid., 1:569.

48. *Calendar of the Patent Rolls, Preserved in the Public Record Office: Edward IV, Edward V, Richard III, A.D. 1476–1485* (London: Mackie, for His Majesty's Stationery Office, 1901), entry for 27 January 1485.

49. *Calendar of the Patent Rolls, Preserved in the Public Record Office: Henry VII, Volume I, A.D. 1485–1494* (London: Hereford Times, for His Majesty's Stationery Office, 1914), entry for 28 November 1493.

50. John Leland, *The Itinerary of John Leland, in or about the Years 1535–1543,* ed. Lucy Toulmin Smith, 5 vols. (1907; reprint, London: Centaur, 1964), 4:89. For later references to the almshouse, see Francis Peck, *Academia Tertia Anglicana or The Antiquarian Annals of Stanford* (1727; reprint, East Ardsley, Eng.: EP Publishing, 1979), 12–13, B20, F11–12; *The Victoria County History of Lincolnshire* 2:234–35, entry 100, "The Hospital of All Saints, Stamford"; Rotha

Mary Clay, *The Medieval Hospitals of England* (1909; reprint, London: Frank Cass, 1966), 83, 269; and David Knowles and R. Neville Hadcock, *Medieval Religious Houses: England and Wales* (1953; reprint, London: Longmans, Green, 1971), 308.

51. Sources checked include Margaret Bowker, *The Secular Clergy in the Diocese of Lincoln, 1495–1520*, Cambridge Studies in Medieval Life and Thought, n.s., 13 (Cambridge, Eng.: Cambridge University Press, 1968); A. B. Emden, *A Biographical Register of the University of Cambridge* (Cambridge, 1963) and *A Biographical Register of the University of Oxford to A.D. 1500*, 3 vols. (Oxford, 1957–59); C. W. Foster and A. H. Thompson, eds., "The Chantry Certificates for Lincoln and Lincolnshire, Returned in 1548," *Associated Architectural Societies' Reports and Papers* 37.1–2 (1923–26): 100–06, 250–51 (nos. 115–23); John Le Neve, *Fasti Ecclesiae Anglicanae, 1300–1541: I. Lincoln Diocese*, comp. H. P. F. King (London: Athlone Press, 1962); *Lincoln Wills, 1271–1530*, 2 vols., Lincoln Record Society, no. 5 (1914) and no. 10 (1918); and Peck, *Academia*.

# The Myrour of Recluses

# [Part 1: Four Motivations for the Vocation

## PREFACE]

["See your vocation" (1 Cor. 1:26), o dearly beloved recluses, and so that we may understand more clearly and
more successfully your calling (you as much by attending
as I by exhorting), in the beginning let us sincerely invoke
the aid of the blessed Trinity, of the Father, the Son, and
the Holy Spirit, who are one God Almighty, wisest and kind-
est, so that in this work it may inspire my heart, direct my
speech, and govern my hand in writing. O sweetest Lord
Jesus Christ, for whose love recluses customarily allow
themselves to be enclosed forever, desiring above all things
to fulfill your will, may you now mercifully deign to show
me, your]

| [mes]sager, þouȝ I vnworthi be, what is moost plesaunt to | 1
the in her lyf, or what may be moost expedyent or speedful
vnto her helthe.

O benigne Ihesu, O singuler and only "wardeyn and keper
of men" [Job 7:20] & her saueour, se the syghinges of thi | 5
caytifes & wrecches, se the desires of thi chosen folk, se
the periles of temptacions, and schew vn-to me what I schal
telle on-to hem, & ordeigne and purveye þat that I schal
wryte vn-to þe preisynge, glorie, and honour of þiself. Now,
Holy Goost, hyl[e] and poure out on vs thin oyle of thi | 10
mercy, opne the welle of thi pite and of thi grace, and put
in vs lyȝt of trouþe & science to knowe how & of whom
bien the recluses of oure tyme callid vn-to þe solitarie lyf
in which they lyuen.

Now wheþre, as it ys drawen and gadrid out of the lyues | 15
and stories of seyntes, of hem that chesen this lyf of reclus,
ffourfold may be þe causes, motif, and sterynge or enten-

3

cion principal? The firste mai be cause and entencion of
lyuynge at her [1v] owen wyl, with-oute labour. The secunde
ys wil of gret and feruent repentaunce. The thride ys purpos    20
to eschewe the oportunite of synnynge in commune defautes
or blames. And the ferthe ys desyr of on-tendynge the more
frely to dyuyn contemplacion and only to the worschip and
preysynge of Oure Lord God.

The firste cause or entencion longith to wrathful and    25
sleuthi folk, as yt schewyth in some þat nat han profityd in
this manere of lyuynge. The secunde cause and entencion
ys conuenient to folk contryt and wel consciencyd, as yt
schevvyth of Tayse, þat was vnhonest of hir body, Marie
Egypcian, and oþir mo. The þridde cause or entencion    30
acordiþ to dredful folk and simple, as were in þe bygynnynge
Paule, the firste heremyte, and Hyllarion. And the ferthe
cause or entencion ys conuenient and fittynge to deuout and
spiritual folk, as was in wyldirnesse aftir þe Ascencion [2r]
of Oure Lord, Marie Maudeleyne, which "chees þe beste    35
paart" [Luke 10:42].

Therfor, aftir the forseid foure causes or entencions, þe
lyf & clepynge of euery reclus, as I trowe, may be dece[r-
n]yd, how and of what spiryt it is bygonne. And therfor, +
ech of þis foure schal singulerly be tretyd.    40

## [CHAPTER 1: TO LIVE AT LIBERTY AND WITHOUT LABOR]

To some it happyth, as I seide aboue, to be led by spirit
of errour to lyue solitarily, þat, of deuocion and almesse of
trewe Cristen peple, þei may þe more ple[n]teuously haue
temporal goodes wherof to lyue & dyspende þan thei were
likly to haue in any other maner of lyuynge, and that, in    45
vigilijs, fastinges, orisons, and oþir occupacions, þei may
ordeigne & dispose hem aftir her wil, fleynge, in-as-mochil
as thei may of hir voluptuus sleuthe or sleuthi fleschly lust,
þe ʒok of obedience and bodili laboures and anguysches of
þis lyf, as some religiouses now þese dayes enforcein hem    50
to do. For the whiles þei be sumwhat restreynyd of her
lustes, aftir her holi obseruaunces of her religion, as in

foode, [2v] cloþinge, occupac[i]ons disconuenient, & excessyf solaces; þei wyncen, grucchen, & wiþstonden in alle
þe weyes & maneres þat þei can & may, demynge her souer-    55
eynes froward, euyl-willid, or vndiscreet, and but þei be suffrid sumwhat to lyue aftir þe arbitrement and doom of her
owen wil, þei fleen f[ro] her ordre as children of perdicion
& procuren and suen an exempcion or sum oþer liberte, and
þat nat withouten scripule or wem of conscience, as to be    60
þe popes chapleyns or byscopes nullatenses, þat þei mowe
in þat wyse frely & wilfully entende to her vnliefful lustys
and so, be consequence, be lappyd & inuoluyd in "þe feendes snares" [2 Tim. 2:26], with-oute lettynge or inpediment
of any whyght.                                              65

Now wheþir þei ben nat conformynge to þese þat desiren
a solitarie lif þat taken it nat fyrst ne principaly for þe loue
of God, but for to leede her lyf aftir her lust? Treuly, I trowe
ʒis. But lyʒtly ne certeynly may it nat be knowyn which
þo bien. [3r] Natheles, lat euery mannes conscience deeme    70
"wiþ-oute feynynge" [Wisd. 7:13] for what cause rathest he
hath chosen a solitarie lyf, and what was his meuynge or
stirynge entent principal. ʒif þat [þe] first & þe moost motif
were reste or any othir temporel solace, as fredam to haue
his owen wil, sustentacion and beryng vp of cosyns and     75
frendes, or sotil adquisicion or purchasynge of temporel
thinges, euery swychoon lat hym dreede, rewe, & forþinke
yt, and fram hennys-forþ leet hym sytte and change his purpoos, sette his final entent principaly in the loue and seruise
of God, and caste abak al inordinat affeccions. In this man-   80
ere by þe grace of God may thei chaunge her clepynge from
evyl in-to good, from þe wrong in-to ryʒt, and fro vices into
vertues, seyinge vnto God faithfully wiþ Seynt Iob, "Thow
schalt calle me & I schal ansuere þe. Thow schalt putte forth
thi ryʒt hand vnto þin handwerk" [Job 14:15]. As þouʒ he    85
scholde sey openly, "Ffor þat I now coueyte to repente me
of my synnes [3v] and erroures þat bien passid, thow God
Almyʒtyful schalt 'calle me' by grace, 'and I schal ansuere
þe' be þe obseruaunce and kepynge of þi wil; but to þe
entent þat I may suffice to performe þat good deede, 'þu     90
schalt putte forþ þe ryʒt hand' of þi spiritual help & conser-
uacion to me þat am 'þe werk of þin handes' to voide fro

me the wykkyd custom of superflu delectacion in gay and
precious cloþinges, in delycat metys and drynkes, and in
oþer maner vses necessarie to man, and also in rychesses,        95
flesly freendes & cosyns, in veyn and vnclene and vnliefful
þouȝtes, & of vnhonest, unprofitable, and ydil talkynges."
    It hath happid recluses nat wiel disposid ne wis, of þe
abundaunce of temporel þinges and þoruȝ hauntynge of
men of diuerse condicion visitynge hem, be ofte sythes de-       100
foulyd & apeyred in her condicions and maneres. This
schewyth of some recluses in þese dayes, nat in wilder-
nesses but in þe citees, þat þei may þere receyue large
almes, wher-of þei may holde greet meynee [4r] and helpe
and promote more largely her kyn and her freendes þan þei       105
myȝte in her oþir estat and lyue more delicatly þan þei were
likly haue doon in seculer plyt. Tho recluses bien ofte vesi-
tid wiþ men and women þat schewen gay & neyce aparail
and cloþi[s] in her syȝt & tellen hem þinges of worldly lust,
as vnclene wordes and vncouenable, & tellen hem tydynges       110
& auentures þat fallen in diuerse contrees, of þe whiche
þinges þo þat remaynen & duellyn in her mynde, þouȝ þei
seme [nat] outward mortel and deedly synnes, ȝet naþeles
inward þei vexen & troublen merueyllously her þouȝtes
and dryuen hem in-to diuerse fantasies, so þat her redynge    115
is þe more vnsauoury, her preier lasse deuout, and al her
meditacion vicious.
    O gentil knyȝtes of Ihesu Crist, o ȝe nurces of perfec-
cion, o secret and priue chamberleyns of Oure Lord Ihesu,
dooþ aftir þe conseil of Seynt Iohan, which seith in this       120
wyse, "Seeth and beholdiþ ȝoure owen self, lest ȝe lese
þat þat ȝe haan [4v] doon and wrouȝt" [2 John 1:8]. Fforsothe, yt appertenyth nat to youre estat to lyue delicatly, as
to receyue poure folk & pilgrymes; wiþholde meyne passynge to seruauntȝ; bringe forth ȝoong folk custummably,    125
as in multitude or for hyre; or to bere the charge of helpynge
of ȝoure cosyns and frendes. But ȝif it happe þat a vertu-
o[u]s persone, be yt cosyn or ellis, þoruȝ infortune of þe
world be driuen to scharp meschief or pouert and hath but
smal or no confort of socour or relief, thanne ys yt good       130
and meritorie to releue suych a persone. And ȝet, ȝe be
more hoolden to releue ȝoure blood, ȝif he be vertuous þan

an-oþer strange persone, þouȝ it be vertuous & meritorie to
releue hem bothe.

Also, ȝe scholde nat be ocupyed wiþ vnhonest or veyn     135
wordes or talkynges. B[ut] ȝe scholde ȝow content wyth
mene foode and sustenaunce & symple cloþinge for ȝoure
body, aftir þe conseyl of þe apostil, ente[n]dynge hooly to
þo þinges þat apertienen and longen to þe helþe of ȝoure
soules; let n[e] ire disturble or lette [5r] ȝow fro the conty-     140
nuance of vertuous werkes, ne slouþe tarie ȝow þat vnmesurably ys accus[tu]med and wont to tempte ydyl folk. As
for þe remedie of sleuthe, ȝe may concidre sondri creatures.
Byhoold now and se how þat þe heuenely speeres with alle
her planetes and sterres, the eyr with foules and briddes,     145
the watir wiþ fyssch and oþir þinges vnresonable ovir þe
[erþe] be meuyd & werken aftir þe lawe ȝeuen and taken
vnto hem of nature, to do plesaunce vnto her Creatour, for
þouȝ þei han noon hope to haue eternel blisse, ȝet do they
alwei her operacion and werk, mynistrynge euyr her seruise     150
vnto þe behoue of mankynde, ȝeuynge ensample in al þat
þei may to perseuere in good werkes to plesaunce and lykynge of her God.

Now, [for]þan, whether ȝe þat been professid in þe lyf of
moost perfeccion schul continue good exercise wiþ glad     155
herte for þe loue of God, aftir þe scripture þat seiþ, "Lat
euery man duuelle to-ward God in þe same callynge þat he
ys clepyd" [1 Cor. 7:20]? And þus, by good [5v] perseuer-
aunce, "seeth now ȝoure callynge and clepynge" [1 Cor.
1:26].     160

## [CHAPTER 2: TO PERFORM GREAT AND FERVENT PENANCE]

The secunde cause and entencion principal of recluses
may be feruent wil of repentaunce and forþenkynge al þe
terme of þis lyf of þe offences & synnes þat þei haan doon.
And þei þat so contynue & perseuere in her purpoos, yt is
to hope and to leue þat thei be callyd of þe Holy Goost,     165
aftir þe sentence of Ihesu Crist þat seyth, "I cam nat to
penaunce to calle ry[ȝt]wys folk, but synneres" [Luke

5:32]. But netheles, to hem þat chesen þis man*ere* of lyf
solitarie, ful needful ys a p*ru*dent circu*m*speccion (þat is to
sey, to take good avis and delib*era*cion in this caas), lest of      170
lyȝt and sodeyn assent of þe herte, w*ith*-oute wys p*u*ruey-
aunce or forsyȝt, þei chese the hardnesse of þat lyf &
knytte or bynde hem þerto, or make as [w]ho seyth a p*ro*-
messe or byheste þer-to be symple avow, by þe stirynge of
"þe angel Sathenas, þat ofte-tymes + transfigureth hym in-      175
to þe aungel of lyȝt" [2 Cor. 11:14] and sleyȝli vndir þe
col*ou*r of holynesse areiseth þe herte of sum vnstable p*er*-
sone, excitynge [6r] hym to entr*e* in-to þat heyg charge, &
aftirward makeþ hem falle adoun more p*er*ilously, as I haue
knowen yt hath to some, in-to her p*er*petuel desolacion.      180

This p*er*fyt and holy lyf ys in hem þat, by þe abundance
and plente of Goddys grace, by long stryf and fyȝtynge
agayn temptacions, han p*er*fitly ouyrcome alle her passions
and han quenchid alle inordinat affeccions, as fer as it is
possible to any pylgry*m* of þis lyf p*re*sent; and now thei      185
alone suffisen to fiȝte ageȝn alle temptacions & han goten
& purchased hem g*ra*ciously so mochel swetnesse of þe love
of God & of contemplacion þat thei sauour*e* nat in erþely
thinges, but delyten hem & reioycen hem in heuenely þin-
g*es*. Suych folk han no nede to þe doctrine or techynge of      190
man; I write to noon suyche, but al-only to i*m*perfit folk
þat desiren to ascende and clymbe to þe heyest degr*e* of
p*er*feccion, for vnto suiche is a solitarie lif ful p*er*ilous, and
it is no wonder whan a ma*n*nys soule ys put to [6v] fyȝt
continuely vn-to the deeth agayn al possible temptacions &      195
agayn þe horrible oost of wykkyd spiritis. And þerfore, this
maner of lyf askyth and requireth a p*er*fyt man, wher-of
seith þe Wise Man ryȝt thus, "I foond," he seyth, "o man
among a *thousand*" [Eccles. 7:29].

And therfor, who-so desireth a solitarie lyf, willinge to      200
repente and rewe his offenses & giltes, nouþ*er* wole I conseile hym to take it on hyur, ne stire ne rede hym to leue it,
ffor I woot nat by what spirit he is led, ne what meuyth ne
steryth hym, but I conseile and rede in this man*ere*. Ffirst,
let hym schewe his p*u*rpos to to or þre p*er*sones to-gidere      205
þat bien discret and good lyuers þat mowe diligently and
bisily examyne his entent wiþ alle p*er*tinent circumstaunces.

And þoruȝ her assent & conseil, lat [hym] proue hym-self
continuely al an hool ȝeer, lyuynge in alle þinges lik or
moore streytly þan a reclus is holde to doo, but ȝet na-          210
theles, lat hym nat in þe meen-tyme determyne his wyl [7r]
in that, ne make noon avow, and whan this ȝeer is al fully
passid, þanne prey euery day the Fadir of mercy þat he
vouchesauf to enspire hym what ys best vn-to the helthe of
his soule and finali what schal moost plese [God]. And ȝif     215
he duelle and contynue in his desir as he dide byforn & þat
þe conseil of discreet men conforme & assente vn-to hym
by good and ripe avys an[d] deliberacion, þane lat hym
stablissche his wil in this caas & knytte vp his purpoos &
take þat lyf or make his avow þerto, trustynge in þe grace       220
& mercy of his God. Oþir-wyse þan þus or lik to þis wolde
I nat conseile þe lyf of recluses to chese or avow. Natheles,
aftir a symple avow is maad or suych lyf admittid & taken
with + necessarie deliberacion & avys, it schal be kept vnto
þe ende+, o[n] peyne of eternel and euere-lastinge          225
dampnacion.

Therfore, to alle þo þat ben professyd in þat lyf is it charitable to putte forth or schewe þe exortacion of þe [7v] apostel, wher he seyth, "I byseche + ȝow þat ȝe walke & go
worthili in þe callinge in which ȝe ben cleept" [Ephes. 4:1].     230
Diuers is þe callynge of sondry folk aftir diuerse ȝeftes of
God, wheþir suich be goodes of þe body, or goodes of þe
soule, or goodes temporel, or contrarie of hem, which
happyth to be goodes by accidence. þo maken folk in diuerse
kyndes stroong or feeble, symple or prudent, poore or          235
myȝti. Ffor some arn callyd to Goddys seruise wiþ helþe
and strengþe, some wiþ febilnesse & syknesse; some wiþ
good & natural complexion, some with euyl complexion;
some with many vertues, some wiþ fewe; some wiþ riches,
some with pouert; some wiþ wrecchidnesses and infortunes,     240
and some with al manere of prosperite. Alle þese with-outen
doute, ȝif they come fro God and nat of mannys vice, schullen more profite finaly to her possessoures þan scholde her
contraries, ȝif thei vse hem wiel.

"O þe heyȝnesse of þe wysdom and science of God"              245
[Rom. 11:33], O þe gracious puruey[a]nce of Oure [8r] Creatour, O þe excellent mercy of Oure Lord God, þat clerly

seeþ byforn alle þinges þat schullen folwen and been possible to falle & calleþ euery wyght so to helthe, as to estat, condicion, & oþir circumstaunces, ʒif þat thei hem-self putte noon obstacle ne lettynge, þat þei may sufficiently be sauyd & eschewe þe peril of dampnacion, inso-mochel þat alle maner harmes þat fallen to Goddes chosen peple schullen profite to ay-lastynge helþe: "To hem þat loven God, alle þinges werkyn in-to good or werkyn wiel and taken good effect, to hem þat aftir hir purpos bien callid seyntes" [Rom. 8:28]. Fforsoþe aftir her purpoos þei ben callyd "seyntes" þat ben predestinat to God to euerlastynge lyf. Suich folk ben nat only callyd outward by ensample, by holy scripture, or by predicacion, but also by enspirynge & grace of perseuerance fynaly in charite. In suich wyse ben folk chosen in comparison of al a multitude which is clepid. Here-of beryth Crist wytnes. He seith, "Many ben callyd & fewe ben chosen" [Matt. 20:16]. [8v] Fforsoþe, "tho that God hath predestyned, he hath callyd hem so; and wham he clepte in þat manere, hem, ʒif þat [þei] falle, he iustifieth bi grace of penaunce; and wham þat he iustifieþ so, hem he magnifieþ be habundaunce and plente of grace and vertu" [Rom. 8:30], aftir þe sentence of þe apostel þat seith þus.

　　As many as ʒe been þat ben clepid to do penaunce in testat of perfeccion of recluses, "beth ioyful and gladiþ" in God [Matt. 5:12], trustynge stedefastly on his grace and mercy, "þat ʒoure names bien wretyn in heuene" [Luke 10:20]. Wherfor ordeigneth and purueyeth ʒow euyrmore a faget of alle ʒoure offences and giltes byforn ʒoure eyen of ʒoure wil & of ʒoure herte, remembrynge of þe greet mercy of God & his manyfold grace doon & schewed ⁺ vn-to ʒow and profred frely to hem þat been penytent & repentaunt with-outen ende, and for þe offense of God & for his excellent mercy medlith to-gidre sorwe with ioye, & gladnesse with heuynesse. Thus, ofte þe deuocion of a perfyt [9r] contricion tolliþ out & bringiþ out gladsum teres and wepynge gladnesse, whil þat þe ende & entent of þe greet desir comeþ out & stillith out be þe een swete dropes of deuocion. And whoso-euyr haþ þis precious licour, which is helþe of þe synful soule, he wolde nat gladly chaunge yt for a gret kynges tresour, ffor aftir þe bittir teres of suych

250

255

260

265

270

275

280

285

contricion longe exercysed & vsyd, entriþ þe suetnesse of
þe loue of God, which loue ys more þan man can deeme or
gesse. O who schal make me partyner of suych holy teres?            290
Who schal "wassche" my felþes "wiþ þe watres of Syloe"
[John 9:7, 11], þat goon wiþ silence & stilnesse, syn I am al
drye? "I preie & biseche ȝow" [Song Sol. 2:7, 3:5], þerfore,
þat þoruȝ grace "drawen watres in ioye of þe welles of Oure
Saueour" [Isa. 12:3], for þe hy mercy of Oure Lord God,            295
"whan it is wiel with ȝow, remembrith & þenketh on me"
[Gen. 40:14] & departiþ with me charitably of þe leeste
droopes þat fallen fro ȝow of þe abundaunce of ȝoure blysful teres.

More-ovir, I desire þat ȝe wacche [9v] bisili agayn þe            300
temptacions of þe feend, þat noþing sleuthe or lache ouyr-
mochil þe stiburn hardnesse of ȝoure lyf vndir colour of
fals necessite, ne noþing augmente or ecche it ouyr ȝour
force or myȝt, but aftir þe doom & arbitrement of discrecion, chastise & nursche ȝoure body in diuerse tymes, þat            305
it be soget on þat o side to þe commaundement of ȝoure
spirites & suffisaunt on þat oþir part to performe & fulfille
þe labour enioyned to þe body. & þerfor in ȝour greet febilnesse or infirmite ordeynyth or purueyth ȝow wysly necessarie recreacion & refresschinge to þe body, & whan it is            310
revigured (þat is to seyn, þat it haþ cauȝt agayn his strengþe
and is restored to helþe), þanne myȝtyly resumeþ and takeþ
agayn þe armes of spiritual knyȝthode, þenkynge þat ȝe
schullen nat only continue ȝoure meritorie & medful
werkes for ȝoure-self, but also for othir soules þat suffren            315
in purgatorie, & for alle Cristen peple to [10r] + þe which
ȝe ben obliged and holden be þe lawe of charite. O who
can deeme o[r] gesse what turment þo soules suffren þat
ben in purgatorie, whos peyne ys mochel moore greuous
þan any peyne þat is in this lyf? Seynt Gregori hadde +            320
leuer chose þe contynuel feueres while he lyued here þan
suffre þre dayes þe peyne of purgatorie. O ther nys tonge
þat can expresse the smert of þe peynes of helle, which ben
insuffrable for þei han noon ende. "Therfor, yt is ful holy
and hoo[l]sum to preye for hem þat ben deede, þat þey may            325
ben dissoluyd and vnknet of her synnes" [2 Macc. 12:46],

and also for to preie for þe synful men þat lyuen here þat
þey may [be] preseruyd and kept fro þe peynes of helle.

These and oþir þinges lik to þese impressith and receyuyth in-to ȝoure myndes, & lat hem styre and meeue ȝow          330
to contynue the lyf of perfeccion which ȝe haue taken, la-
bourynge & travaylynge in orisons, wakynges, fastynges,
and alle oþir obseruaunces. And thus by þe grace of Almyȝty [10v] God ȝe "schul perseuere and contynue vn-to
þe ende" [Matt. 24:13], "in þe clepynge which ȝe ben clept          335
vnto" [1 Cor. 7:20]. And in þis wyse by couenable penaunce,
"seeþ ȝoure clepynge and callynge" [1 Cor. 1:26].


## [CHAPTER 3: TO AVOID THE OPPORTUNITY FOR SIN]

The þridde cause or entencion principal of recluses may
be þe purpos to eschewe oportunite or þe occasion & cause
which is wont to induce [or] to leede a man in-to deedly          340
synne. The fyve wyttis of þe body as vn-wys messageres of
mannes herte ben accustumed and wont alwey & ouyral to
recorde in hem-self al þat þei han take and receyuyd, be yt
veyn þinges, or vnprofitable, anoyinge, greuynge, or enclynynge vn-to synne. Therof happith often-sithe þat þei þat          345
ben symple and feerful to falle & to slyppe in-to deedly
synne, whan they byhold & considere her freelte & þe per-
ilys of synnes þat þei ben likly to fallen ine, which take her
bygynnynge of þe fyve wyttys þat sterten here & þere in
þe world wiþ-outen obstacle or bridel, ffor þe moore syker          350
eschewynge of alle þese [11r] periles, of a prudent ferue[nt]-
nes[s]e or of a feruent prudence, thei werkyn aftir þe conseyl of Salomon, seyinge in this manere, "[Call] prudence
þi love or þi freend" (þat ys to seyn, þe warþeyn & kepere
of þi wyl) [Prov. 7:4].          355
O which and how greet prudence ys askyd and requyred
to þe kepynge of þe wyt of þe syȝte, þat inpressith & en-
pryntyth in þe herte of a persone what þat he byholdeþ &
seeþ as beaute of creatures, preciosite of cloþinge, schap,
port, and werkynge, which engendryn concupiscence of þe          360
flesch & nurschen lustes of þe body þat causen ofte a man

to do wykkydly. Wheþir þat þe syȝte of [Dalida] were nat
þe cause of þe ruyne or fallynge of Sampson þat excedyd
and passyd alle men in strengthe? Wheþir þe syȝte of
straunge wommen turnyd nat and chaungyd þe herte of          365
Salomon þe wyse? Wheþir þe syȝte of Vries wyf baþinge
her maade Dauyd þe holy prophete to falle in-to cursyd
avoutrie & man-slauȝtre? What þing engendred þefte &
stelþe or [11v] vnlyefful coueytise in Achor, but þe syȝte
of precious þinges? What maade oure modyr Eve to synne      370
but þe lycourous look of þe deffendyd or forboden tree, and
what maade þe children of Israel more prest or redy to doon
ydolatrie þan þe syȝte of þe rytes and þe lawes of þe hethen
peple and communycacion or spekynge wyth suych folk þat
honureden and worschipeden feendes? Therfor, þe prophete     375
Dauyd preieþ Oure Lord God & seyth þus, "Torne awey
myn eyen, lest þei seen or byholde vanyte" [Ps. 118:37].

Moore-ovyr, þe ere souketh and receyuyth al þat euyre
he heryth of þe slym & felþe of synne, as songes & karoles
of love; foul & vnclene speches; streyve, accusacions, bla-      380
mynges; wordes of detraccion or bacbytynge; wordes of en-
vye, pride, auarice; glosynges and lesynges. Loo, alle suych
þinges þorugh her wykkyd ensample mowe lyȝtly drawe
and stirie a man to synne, as seyth þe prophete Dauyd: "I
am maad," he seyth, [12r] "as a vessel þat ys loost, for I      385
haue herd þe accusacion or blamynge of many folk þat duell-
lyn in þe circuyt o[r] compas" (þat is to seyn, of hem þat
duellen aboute me) [Ps. 30:13–14]. O blessyd is þe ere þat
ys so prudently disposid þat he openeþ nat þe ȝates agayn
suych vnleefful noyses; & ys schyt & spered agayn þe vo-      390
luptuous or lusty melodyes of the world; & ys stoppyd agayn
alle þo sounes of temptacions, but in-as-mochel as ys possible to hym þat lyueth in þis valeye of wrecchidnesse; &
kepith h[y]m a-feer from alle worldly vanytes, as yt schewith
by euydence & tokne of recluses (& naamly of anchoresses,     395
þat bien more streytly closed þan oþir religious men & wommen, enclosed + in her houses be leue of he[r] souereyns
and in alle tymes at her souereyns wyl).

Swych ancres & ankeresses ben more sekyrly conseruyd
& kept fro þe peryls of þe bodyly wyt of touchynge, by þe      400
which entriþ þe lust of lecherie in sondry wyse, as wiel

naturel or kyndely as vnnaturel or [12v] vnkyndely, which
wiþ-draweþ a man fro vertu & maketh hym abhomynable
to angeles, "hatful to God" [Rom. 1:30], & alieneth hym or
maketh hym straunge from al grace. Alle suych spices of          405
lecherie ben fer from an ancresse, but ȝif it happe per-caas
+ of a voluptuous or lusty delectacion or delyt of þe herte
in vnliefful þouȝtes; [& ȝif þei ben] loonge abydynge [&]
ben engendringe + a consent to delyte in þat same, þan
wiþouten doute yt induceþ a man in-to deedly synne. &          410
ȝif he contynue suych delyt wakynge vn-to þe tyme þat þe
voluptuous pollucion of þe body folwe, þan ys þer doon a
manere o[r] spice of "lecherie agayn kynde," which is callyd
in Latyn of þe apostyl "molicies" [1 Cor. 6:10]. Now be yt
no displesaunce to ȝow þat I expresse þus vnhonest þinges          415
in my wrytynge to folk of clene & perfyt lyf, ffor where is
possibilite of temptacion, þer ys a prudent enformynge of
resistence or wiþstondynge ful necessarie & meedful. Ffor
þe trewe storie + seyth þat þer was [13r] an hermyte hoolden
a ful holy man which custummably vsyd þis sinne & was          420
vexid þerwith þis synne of "molicies" and chargid yt nat in
his conscience as for synne and repentyd hym nat be contricion ne confession; wherfor he was sodeynly ravyssched &
taken wiþ a feend and neuyr apperyd aftyr, which dede, as
I suppose, was schewyd of God in ensample & to þe doc-          425
tryne of oþir folk, to make hem euyr wiþstonde in al her
myȝtes suych manere of voluptuous delyt & neuere ȝeue
her assent þerto, and ȝif þei falle at any tyme in suych caas,
as God kepe hem þerfro, to be sory and repentaunt þerof,
and so for þe victorie of a scharp & greuous spirituel ba-          430
taylle, þei may aftir þis lyf be coroned in ioye.

  Suych a corone may "Cristes knyth" deserue [2 Tim. 2:3],
wiþdrawynge hym fro excessyf & outrageous lustes of
smellynge & tastynge þat ben engendryd of sauoures &
odoures delicates, in metys & drinkes, & in spices aromatik,          435
in sote sauour of floures & fruytes, [13v] & in vsynge of all
suych nurschynge þinges þat prouoken diuerse spices of
glotonye and by processe drawen þe wrecchid man in-to
dulnesse & sleuthe or excite & styre hym vn-to fles<c>hly
vnclennesse.          440

Suich contynuel occasions of synnes, þat comen of þe
fyve wyttes in a seculer lyf, many of oure olde fadres were
wont to fle & eschewe; þerfor, þei desired & coueytid to be
closyd in a streyt place where-as they myȝten haue oon
necessarie foode and cloþinge. Alle suych folk, as yt is dee-  445
[m]yd & leeuyd, ben enspiryd with þe Holy Goost, & as
who seyth, been callyd of God, to whom acordith verraily
þe word of þe apostel, þat seith in this manere, "God callyd
vs nat in-to clennesse, but in-to satisfaccion" [1 Thess. 4:7].
And therfore, ȝe recluses, "seeþ so ȝoure clepynge" [1 Cor.  450
1:26] in-to contin[u]el eschewynge of synnes.


## [CHAPTER 4: TO PURSUE THE CONTEMPLATION AND PRAISE OF GOD]

The ferþe cause or entencion principal of recluses may
be desyr to entende moore frely to þe contemplacion of God
and [14r] to hys honour and p[r]esynge aftir þe conseil of
þe prophete Dauyd, where he seith þus: "Taak heede &  455
seeth" [Ps. 45:11], "for Oure Lord ys so[o]te and esy" [Ps.
33:9]. That entendynge desyren þei þat felen in hem-self be
experience or by preef so mochel mercy of God þat, while
þei entenden nat, ne "medlen wiþ worldly needes" [2 Tim.
2:4], þei may fully, feruently, & deuoutly byholde God &  460
ȝeue & ȝeelde hym hertly þonkynges of alle hys ȝeeftes.
And þerfore, yt is no meruayl þouȝ þei desire & coveyte
g[r]eetly to flee & eschewe þe worldly besynesses, for þis
entendaunce or besynesse, þis holy ydilnesse, þis profitable
reste, ys wont comunely to be let be þouȝtful besynesse of  465
þe herte, by occupacion of þe wyt, and by bodyly labour in
needes of þe world.
Ffor experyence techith in þre parties of þe same contem-
platif lyuynge þat þe besynesse which þat þe herte haaþ
aboute temporal occupacion lettiþ þe fruyt of contemplatyf  470
lyf, and þat ys to seyn in preyere, meditacion, & redynge.
Ffirst, as [14v] to preyere, in-as-mochil as þe herte ys wiþdrawen fro þo þinges þat þe tonge spekyth, þenkynge or
musynge of oþir veyn and inpertynent þinges, y-doute it nat,
euery man woot wiel þat þe þouȝt which a man hath in-  475

forth, be yt love or hate, ioye or sorwe, steriþ so gretly þe
herte as for þe tyme þat yt suffreth no hertly mynde of
Goddys seruise to duelle or abyde with hym. Of þo þat
seruen God in þat wyse, þe prophete spekyth scharply in
þe persone of God and seith þus: "This peple worschepyth     480
me wiþ her tonges, but her herte ys fer fro me" [Isa. 29:13,
Matt. 15:8, Mark 7:6]. As touchinge deuout meditacion, yt
schewyth of lyk euydences þat it is abreggyd & lettyd &
wyttirly wiþdrawen in besy studie & musynge of puruey-
aunce of erþely þinges. And as touchinge holy redynge, yt     485
schewyth also þat hertly besynes aboute temporal þinges
often-sithe byreueþ a man as wel wyl as myʒt of study-
[i]nge, in-so-mochel þat he þat greetly settith his herte in þe
besynesse of þe world, often- [15r] sithe in redynge or her-
ynge of holy scriptures hys mynde is al afeer fro þe wordes     490
and þenkeþ nat on hem.

   More-ovir, þat þe occupacion of þe wyt lettiþ þe werkes
of contemplacion, wytnessyth holy wryt þat seith þus: "The
body þat is corrupt greuyt[h] þe soule, and an erthely inhab-
itacion þrestith dovn þe wyt, þenkynge many þinges" [Wisd.     495
9:15]. As who seyth, "The wyt þat is bysily occupyed aboute
erþely þinges ys so vexed & troubled with hem þat [it] draw-
ith to he[m] or erþely þinges þe affeccions of þe soule, which
ys knyt and bounden to þe bodi." The trouthe of þis may
lyʒtly be schewy[d] þus: lo, naturaly þe wyt representiþ to     500
þe soule to entende to þat þat þe wyt ys excityd or steryd
vnto and to wiþdrawe hym fro þe goode þouʒtes þat he
hade byforn, & þerof is it þat i[n] noyse, or in companye,
or in ope[n] syʒt, or in open place in which many sensible
þinges apperen, þe herte ys withdrawen fro preyere and     505
meditacion & redynge, [15v] which frely wolde entende to
contemplacion & continue þere-ine in silence, in secret, and
[in] derk places. Therfore, þe lasse þat þe þouʒt ys oc-
cupied in bodyly goodes, inso-mochel is it more apt or redy
to know spy[ri]tuel þinges. The seyntes weryn nat woont to     510
receyue of God vysyons or reuelacions of hyd þinges—of
God or of heuenly þinges or of þinges þat scholden come
or falle—but it were ouþer in slepynge, whan þat þe vsage
of þe wyttis ys wiþdrawen for a tyme, or as þat yt were in

a rauisschynge, whan þe herte or þe þouȝt considereth nat 515
þe sensible þinges standinge or beynge oboute. As Seynt
Pouel, þat was "rauysschid in-to þe þrydde heuene," he
wyste nat wheþir he was "wiþ-ine his body" or "wiþ-oute
his body" [2 Cor. 12:2].

It is also to schewe, forþermore, þat þe labour of þe body 520
lettiþ ofte a man fro goostly werkes. Al-be-it þat þe bodyly
labour (which ys taken in places & tymes couenable, for
charite, for obedyence, or getynge of necessarie lyf- [16r]
lode, or for cloþinge, or dreiuynge a-way of sleuþe or ydyl-
nesse) be necessarie, meritorye, & byhouely, ȝet natheles, 525
whan yt excedith or passeþ the boundes, it abeteþ & lettiþ
þe profit of spiritual werkynge, as yt schewiþ in hem þat
labouren & trauaylen by-cause of coueytise or setten hertes
ouyr-mochel in suych labour & besynesse, as dooþ þe moost
partie of folk þat occupyen hem bysily in suych cas and 530
herto putten al her diligence, which comunely lettiþ &
sleutheeþ þe werkes & deedes of contemplacion. & þerfore
often-siþes þe merveylous + mercy of Oure Lord God en-
spirith feble and symple, syke folk, þat bien nat apt ne disposyd to worldly werkes, to take hem vn-to lyf of 535
contemplacion, & wondirly werkiþ in hem by þe abundaunce or plente of his myȝty grace, as þe apostel seyth:
God calleþ "þo þinges þat ben nat" as "tho þinges þat ben,"
"and þe seke & þe feeble þinges of þe world haþ God chosen
for to confunde & scheende alle stronge þinges" [1 Cor. 540
1:28]. [16v] That is to say, to make vmble & meke þe myȝti
men & wyse & greete men, lest þat þei scholde ouyrmochel
presume or take vp-on hem trustynge [on] her owene
strengþes and myȝtes, but þat + þey receyve yt meekly as
ȝeuen to hem of þe grace of God only, while þei seen þat 545
þei þat ben nat so wyse as þei, ne so besy in worldly occupacion, do moore plesaunce to God þan þey doon & abounde
in vertues by a more plenteuous grace. Wher-of, aftir þe
sentence of þe apostel, he seyth þat þe predestinacion of a
man to euere-lastynge lyf ys "nat of þe meryt or meede of 550
a man or of his werkes, but of God þat calliþ hym" [Rom.
9:12].

And þerfore, who-so-euere þat chesiþ a solitarie lyf &
receyuyth in-to hym þe Holy Goost by grace and mercy

and schappyth hym to *con*serue & kepe þe feruent heete of      555
deuoc*i*on, it ys to leeve stedefastly þat he ys callyd to þat
estat by þe Holy Goost. And so, ȝe recluses, by þe *grac*e
and m*er*cy of Oure Lord God ȝeuen & schewyd [17r] to
ȝow, "byholdeþ & seeþ ȝour*e* callynge" [1 Cor. 1:26]

# [Part 2: The Contemplative Life

## CHAPTER 1: FERVENT PRAYER]

Secundely, ȝe recluses schul byholde and seen in þis caas 560
and haue good consideracion wher-to ȝe ben principaly
callyd & clept, for ȝe ben callyd to þe exercise or vsage
[of] contemplatyf lyf, which standiþ namly in þre thinges:
þat is to seyn, in feruent preiere, in deuout meditacion, and
in edificatyf spekynge (þat is to sey, in speche strecchinge 565
vn-to vertu).

A feruent preiere, after þe sentence of seyntes, ys an
ascendynge or reysynge vp [of] þe herte in-to God, askynge
of hym mekly sum-þing þat is necessarie to helþe; wher-of
yt semyth by evydence or tokne þat nedes at þe leest wey 570
in þe bygynnynge of preyere required & askyd þe lyftynge
vp of þe herte in-to God or an entencion & wil to performe
hertly his preyere to þe worschip of God & vn-to þe relees
& socour of þe nede of man. And þis firste e[n]tent, proced-
ynge of charite, makeþ al the [17v] + preyere folwynge 575
meedful, al-be-yt þat þe þouȝt aftyrward be stiryd or set
on temporal þinges or be rauyssched to þenke vnliefful þinges or be drawen apart be veyn & vnprofitabyl þinges, as
yt falleþ contynuely to þo þat ben inperfit, which synnyn
[nat] greuously in þat, ne lakken nat, ne wanten nat þe fruyt 580
of preiere or of orison, but ȝif it so be þat wetyngely &
wyllyngly þei ben wyth-drawen from her purpos. For þouȝ
þat actuel deuocion [which is] passynge meritorie (þat is to
seye, þouȝ deuocion sadly set in God, nat þenkynge on
worldly þinges) be nat in hem þat ben distract of her pur- 585
poos in preyinge, ȝet neþelees þer is in hem an habituel
deuocion (þat is to seyn, as I seyde above, an old rotid
deuocion, willynge to contynue [þerin, þouȝ] distractynge
folwe), which suffiseþ to þe helþe of soule by-cause of þe
firste entent groundyd and ficchid in goodnesse. 590

19

But I trowe þat it falleþ mochel more graciously to þo þat
ben recluses, perfit and lettryd, [18r] which ben wont to
ȝeue þre manere of entendaunces to her preyeres. The firste
is þat þei taken heede to þe wordes of her preyere, leest þei
erre or defayle in hem. The secunde ys þat þei entenden to        595
þe vndirstondynge of þe wordes þat þei mowe sauoure in
hem. The þridde entendaunce is to God for to purchace and
gete þe grace and þe mercy which þat þei askyd in þe tyme
of her preyere. And þis laste & þe þridde entendaunce ys
moost necessarie to hym þat preyeth, and yt may be had of    600
euery vnlettrid man.

ȝif þese þre entendaunces, aftir þe firste entencion of
preyere set & ficchid in goodnesse, be wiþdrawyn þoruȝ
distractynge of hys þouȝt besyde his purpoos, ȝet nat
forþan þer remey[n]eth or duelliþ an habytuel deuocion þat    605
is suffisaunt to helþe. But quenchid ys, in þis caas, þe fer-
uence or heete of actuel deuocion an þe excellence of meedful preyere, which is moost conuenient & acordynge to
recluses & to perfyt folkes. Wherfore, ȝe dere frendes, recluses, [18v] "Seeth, waketh, and preyeth" [Mark 13:33],    610
after þe doctrine of Oure Lord Ihesu Crist. "Seeþ" to how
greet or be hy degre of perfeccion ȝe ben professed.
"Wakeþ" & dooþ ȝoure besy diligence, lest ȝe ben distract
or astonyd in the seruice of God, "& preieth" wiþ actuel
deuocion, þat ȝe may do þe more plesaunt seruice before    615
þe eyen of Goddes magestee & þat ȝoure meryt may be þe
moore echyd or encreced.

The maner of preyere may diuersely eche or encrece deuocion aftir sondry disposicion[s] of man. For, oþirwhile,
the preiere to God in callynge & cr&yinge more steryth deuo-    620
cion; oþirwhile, an orison of þe herte or of þe þouȝt; oþirwhile, an open preiere; oþirwhile, a priue preiere; oþirwhile,
a schort orison, medlyd wiþ oþir honest werkes; oþir-while,
a long preiere; oþir-while, þe preiere þat is maad & ordeyned by God, as is þe Pater Noster; and oþirwhile, an    625
orison maad by man.

Of alle þese þinges, a general reule is to be kept & holden:
þat is to seye, þat þe orisons & preieres to þe which a man
is holden of þe ordynaunce [19r] of Holy Cherche or of hys
souereyns, þat man seye hem & speke hem out fully & holy    630

aftir þe custum of his ordre or his estat. In orisons þat bien
take of a mannes owen wil, lat euery man holde & vse for
a tyme þat manere, þat forme, & þat mesure þat he felyþ
that his deuocion is moost aplyed or vovvyd to & lengest
perseuereþ & endureþ. For þe Dominical preiere (þat is to          635
seyn, þe Pater Noster) ys nat so ordeyned ne maad of God
þat we scholde al-oonly vse þo wordes in oure preiere, but
þat we schul aske non oþir þing in oure preieres þat is sentencialy conteynyd in þat saame. And, forsoþe, it contenyth
& comprehendiþ al þat is necessarie to helþe of mannes          640
soule & of his body. Also, þis is sooþ, wyth-outen doute,
þat be he neuyr so greet and contynuel a synner, ȝif he
aske any-þing of God þat is necessarie to soules helþe, he
schal fynaly haue þe fe[c]t of hys preiere, so þat he wyllyngly agayn þe grace of God putte noon obstacle ne let-          645
tynge by his synne. And [þouȝ] [19v] þe good preyre of þe
synful man be nat merytorie to eternel lyf, ȝit purchaseth
he þerby þe grace of Almyȝti God—nat of hys owen
worthynesse, ne of his desert, but of þe mercy of God & of
his myȝty & excellent goodnesse. And as to þat, þus byhet-          650
yth Crist and seyth, "Alle þinges þat ȝe þat preien asken,
byleueth þat ȝe schullen haue hem, & þei schullen falle vn-
to ȝow" [Mark 11:24]. And þ[is] schul ȝe vndirstonde wiþ
þe forseyd condicions þat bien notyd & expressyd in þe
glose of Luk, as þus: who-so þat louly and perseueryngly          655
or continuely askith any-þing þat is necessarie. So ys yt
vndirstonden.

O þe inestimable and vngessid liberalite & fredoom of
Almyȝti God! O þe grete mercy of Oure Saueour! O þe
merveylously god auenture and þe grace of þe synnere þat,          660
haue he neuere so wykkydly offendyd or greuyd Oure Lord
God, ȝif he wole trustyly turne agayn vnto Hym and for-
sake þe wyl to synne, he may talke with Oure Lord God
Almyȝti whan þat [20r] hym lykyth, by humble & deuout
preiere. He may speke and trete hys needes [wiþ] "þe Kyng          665
of alle kynges" [Apoc. 17:14, 19:16], & wiþ þe Saueour of
al þ<y>s world medle his speche & his wordis. He may
desire what hym lust resonably and haue his askynge. He
may gete pardon of alle his synnes passed, and þoruȝ mercy
be preseruyd and kept from alle periles þat ben to come, &          670

haue here in þis present lyf abundaunce of grace and blisful
glorie endelees, which ys so excellent and so passynge þat
no tonge can telle or expresse yt.

O how mochel þerfore avayleþ þe besy preiere of þe ryȝt-
wys man! Who can or may gesse þe effectua[l] speed, þe 675
value, & þe profyt of þat preiere, namly whan a man preyeth
with plenteuous teres and wyth compunccion of herte?
Suych a preyere purchasyd & gat pardon of forȝeu[en]esse
to Petyr, þat þries forsok Oure Lord God. Suych a preyre
gat grace to Dauyd, þat hadde wrouȝt and doon adeuoutrie 680
and manslauȝtre. And [20v] suych a preiere caused forȝe-
u[en]esse to Marie Magdeleyne of hir fornicacion, and to
the publican askynge mercy. Also, be preyere & penaunce-
doynge, þe people of þe cite of Nynyve eschapid graciously
þe manas and þe þretynge of her destruccion. King Dauyd 685
also eschapyd, of preiere, þe pestilence of peple. Kyng
Ezechias also nat oonly eschaped þe strokes of deeþ, but
he hadde xv ȝeer addid to his lyf, and more-ovir, he addyde
victorie of alle hys enemyes, in-so-mochil þat an Angel of
God slow in a nyȝt an C·iiij<sup>xx·</sup>v·m<sup>l</sup> of his enemys þat anoyed 690
& greued þe peiple of God. Wheþir Moyses þoruȝt his pre-
iere helyd nat the hurtes and woundes of þe Egipciens &
gat victorie to þe children of Israel fyȝtynge agayn Amalec,
while he reysyd vp his hand in deuout preiere? Wheþir also
Iosue, þat ledere was of þe peple, þoru<ȝ>h his preiere 695
maade þe sonne to stonde vnmevable and steryd nat þe
space of a day, þat he myȝte þe better & more frely pursue
[21r] his enemys? Wheþir ek þat Elysee þe prophete þoruȝ
his preiere blynded or maade blynd þe hoost of Cyrye and
ledde hem in-to þe cite of Samarie byforn þe kyng, and how 700
at an-oþir tyme by his preiere Oure Lord God chaced &
droof awey merueylously þe sege of Samarie wiþ a soun
and a noyse of gastnesse? Wheþir eek, by þe preyere of
Helye þe prophete, it reynyd nat on þe erþe þre ȝeer and
vj monþes, and he preyde agayn þat it scholde reyne, & as 705
faste heuen doun schedde reyn plenteuously? Wheþir also
hertly preyere of Salomon gat hym nat his excellent wysdoom? & more-ouyr, þe grettest merveyl of alle þese [ys]
þat þe preiere of þe hethen kyng, þe gret Alysaundre, for
he wolde punsche and chastyse þe offendoures and tres- 710

pasoures agayn þe lawe of God, <sup>+</sup> maade þe hylles of Casp
to renne to-gydres and close & schitte wiþ-ine hem þe mavmettes & rebelles. Also, þe cursyd & wykkyd kyng Achab,
þoruh his herty repentaunce & humble [21v] preyere, God
putte in suspense for his tyme þe vengeaunce þat was ma-          715
naced to hys hous.

Of alle þese þinges, ȝe recluses, be-þenkeþ ȝow, consid-
ereþ, "takeþ heede & seeþ" [Ps. 45:11], how mochil ȝe may
profite as wel to ȝoure-self as to al þe peple, ȝif ȝe perseuere & continue in deuout preiere.                             720

But par caas, sum man myȝte þenke þat no man suffiseþ
to preie wiþ-oute styntynge, ne þat euery contynuel preiere
scholde haue þe fect of his entent. To þat may treuly be
answeryd þat, ȝif a man in tymes to hym compotent and
couenable preye wel actuely his preyere, þouȝ þat aftirward     725
he ete, slepe, or do any oþir þing for þe necessarie [suste]-
nance or refresschynge of þe body (þat he may þe more
strongly serue his God, or for to have [wiþ] his broþer vertuous communycacion & charytable speche), so þat in alle
occupacions þe purpos be set byforn & fynally fycchid in       730
þe seruyse and honour of God, ȝet naþelees, he preyeth
euere habytuely by contynuel desyr and by þe abyt of charite. [Alþouȝ] þe [22r] contynuel preyere [of] many goode
folk take nat oþir-wyse þe effect of hir entent, ȝyt alwey [it
folwyth þat þat preiere is profitable at] þe Jugement of God,  735
to hym for whom yt was preied. For a leche knowyth better
what is profitable to a syk man þan dooþ þe syke man hym-
self. And oþirwyse faileþ neuer þe effect of preiere, but þat
yt schal come in a tyme more couenable, but ȝif þe synne
of hym þat preyeth lette yt, or elles þat it be let by þe       740
contynuance of the deedly synne of hym for whom yt was
preyed.

And þerfore, ȝe recluses, by þese þinges and oþir lyk vn-
to þese, which styren an prouoken a man to feruent preyere,
"by-holdeþ and seeþ [ȝ]oure callynge" [1 Cor. 1:26].           745

## [CHAPTER 2: DEVOUT MEDITATION]

ȝyf lak of deuocion, heuynes, or distr[act]inge lette preiere, þan ful often is yt profitable to drawe ȝow to deuout

meditac*i*on, which may ly3tly by drawen out and contynued
of four*e* þing*es:* þat is to seyn, of þe my3t of G[o]ddys
mageste þat maade al the world of nau3t for [22v] man;          750
of the hy wysdom of sothfastnesse, which gou*e*rneþ moost
ordynatly his affect; and [of] þe greet m*e*rcy of his goodnesse, which delyu*e*rede & bou3te mankynde fro p*e*rpetuel
deeþ; & of p*e*rfyt ry3twysnesse of equite, that schal fynaly
rewarde or punsche eu*e*ry good or wykkyd deede.               755

O thow worthi soule, þow o noble creature, the ymage of
the blessid Trinite, 3if [3ow] byþenke the and remembre
besyly in thi mynde al þe schap of heuene, erthe, and of alle
þinges that bien conteynyd in her circuyt or compaas, þow
mayst vndirstonde and conceyve þat God, þat is hir maker,     760
is almy3ty and his wil in his creatures ys an vnchaunchable
stedefastnesse, the which wyl brou3te forth of nau3t innu-
m*e*rable kyndes of suych þinges þat ben so delectable and
so m*e*rveylously *v*ertuous þat þei passen al out þe intelligence of man in hir p*e*rfyt naturel worchinges.               765

Lo, þu man, lo Almy3ti God maade alle þise thynges for
þe, to s*e*rue þe in vses necessa- [23r] rie, for þat thow
scholdest honour*e* and worschipe hym alwey and 3eue hym
alwey þin herte and ful love above al thinges. And þ*e*rfor,
aftir creac*i*on or makynge of alle oþir þinges, God, by a     770
special p*r*erogatif of love, maade man to þe ymage and lyknesse of hym-self & maade hym a lord of al þat was maad
in the world. Wher-for, lykly yt was þat by þe conseyl of al
þe Trinite (þat is to seyn, of þe Fadir, Sone, and Holy Goost,
þat ben o God and the same God), yt was seyd in þe bygyn-     775
nynge of þe world, "Make we man to þe ymage and oure
liknesse" [Gen. 1:26], as þou3 he scholde sey in this wyse,
"Ry3t as in the Godhede the Sone [is] of the Fadir, and the
[Holy Goost is of the] Fader and of þe Sone togedir, ry3t
so in a maner yt is in a ma*n*nys soule, for of þe memorie or  780
of the mynde of the soule cometh or may come a knowynge
or an vndirstond[yng]e of þe same soule, and of þe mynde
and cnowynge of þe soule to-gydre may come a loue or a
good wyl [23v] to God out of þe same soule. Wherfore, a
man may knowe, as þer ben þre my3t*es* and o substaunce     785
in his soule, ry3th so lyk in a man*er*e þer bien thre p*e*rsones
in the Godhede, and þo þre ben substa*n*cialy on and þe sàme

God." þerfore, this God, that ys þre and oon, ys to be louyd
aftir "þe firste & grettest commaundement" [Matt. 22:38],
"of al þin herte, of al þi soule, of al þi mynde, and of al thi          790
vertu" [Deut. 6:5, Matt. 22:37]: þat is to sey, of al þe myȝt
of thi wyl, of al [þe] myȝt of þi reson or of þin vndirstondynge, or of al þe myȝt of thy mynde, which bien þre parties
of þe ymage of God in þe soule. Also, þow schalt love thi
God þer-wiþ of al thy bodily vertu: þat is to seyn, þat al þe           795
operacion [or] werkynge of þe soule or of þe body be referid
and doon finaly for þe love of God.

& vn-to þis alle creatures, as wel sensible as insensible
creatures, by hir ensample prouoken and styren a man, for
as moche as þat, after þe fyrste ordenance [24r] of God, þei          800
ben in hir contynuel stery[n]ge and trauayles, mynystrynge
and ȝevynge vn-to man nurschynge, solace, and doctryne
alwey to drede, preise, and love, aboven alle þinges, her
Lord and hir Creatour and Maker. [Wheþir] þat þe heuenly
sterynge or meuynge moost ordinatly maad wiþ-outen            805
defaute, the mery noyse of briddes in her swete soun, þe
delyt of floures and fruytes, þe auaunttage and profyt of alle
beestes, þat euery ȝeer ben merveylously renewyd to þe
byhoue of man and folwen withoute fayle þe lawe þat is
ȝouen to hem of nature—& in al þat, þei may enformen &           810
steryn a man to dreede, preise, and love, abouen [alle] þinges, þe excellent myȝt of her Maker, þe hy wysdoom of hir
Conseruatour or Keepere, & þe infynyt or endles goodnesse
of hir Creatour? [ȝis], forsoþe. O þu, þerfor, ymage of God
endued & maad noble aboven alle oþire with a free wyl &           815
choys of reson, ȝif þat þu se in thi-self or in [24v] any oþir
creature, be yt myȝt, prudence, bountee, or honeste, as
blyue referre thou & putte al þat to the preysynge, glorie,
and honour of God, and loue nat that al-only for yt-self, but
principaly and finaly for God. ȝif þow byholde and se in           820
thys world any-þing of defaute, errour, vice, dreede, malice,
wrong, or any-thing vnprofitable or peynful, wyte and ar-
rette al this [to] þe synnes of man, and vnto þe riȝtwys
punschynge or suffraunce of God, þat doþ it for þe synful
scholde be maad hvmble and haue God in dreede, and þat           825
he scholde be punsched and turne aȝen to God & be cor-
rectid and loue his Creatour. And vn-to þis ende, as concey-

lid þe prophete Dauyd & seyde, "Seeth þe werkes of God"
[Ps. 65:5].

Naþeles, the love of God wexiþ more plentevously in man          830
þoruȝ hertly byholdynge of þe werkes of Crist for mannes
profyt, [fro] þe firste salutacion of þe angel to þe Blessyd
Virgine vn-to þe sendynge doun of the Holy Goost. But
among [25r] alle oþer þinges, ofte to remembre hertly on þe
glorious passion of Oure Lord Ihesu moost prikkeþ and ster-          835
ith þe synful man to compunccion of herte; it prouoketh a
man to teres of deuocion; it sterith a man to suffre paciently
scharpe þinges for þe loue of God and strengtheth a man to
withstonde alle temptacions.

Therfore, þow synnere, byhoold and see wiþ þe yen of þi          840
soule how þat wiþ alle þe myȝtes and strengthes, as wiel
of soule as of body, þe Almyȝty Sone of God, þe Kyng of
Glorie, Mercyable Cryst, which is hymself charitee suych
and so greet þat þer nys no tonge that may telle yt, suffrid
strongly for þe to þat entent þat suffisaunt medicyne and an          845
habundaunt satisfaccion may answere to ech of þi synnes
þat thow hast do or mayst do, ȝif þow wylt hertly aske
mercy. Ffor his "soule" was "[tri]sty vn-to þe deeþ" [Matt.
26:38, Mark 14:34], for to heele þe vnleefful gladnesse of þi
fleschly lust. Hys eyes schedden out & droppyd "bitter teres          850
with a loud & greet cry" [Heb. 5:7], [25v] to purchace pardon of forȝeuenesse to þe excesse and offense of þi syȝt.
The eres of þe Kyng of Glorie suffrid blasphemes, disclan-
dres and scornes, fals witnesse and blames, for to ȝeue vn-
to þe þe lore and techynge of pacience to make satisfaccion          855
for þine vnleefful herynges. The mouth of God Almyȝty, in
his mooste þirst, tastide the bittyrnesse of gall and eysil to
wassche awey þe gyltes of þi taast. The noseþirles of his
fayr face smelden þe felþes and vnclenesses and spotil þat
scornful[y] <sup>+</sup> weren þrowen on hym, þat þoruȝ þat þe tres-          860
paas of þi smellynge myȝte have a remedie. And the wyttes
of touch he suffryd in hym by al hys body for þe vsage of
þin vnliefful touch, which body was scharply beeten wyth
knotty scorges, buffettid, crucified, & with a spere & nayles
& þornes þo[r]lede & perside ouyral, & al forbleed, "fro þe          865
sole of þe foot vn-to þe top of his heed" [Isa. 1:6], and his
[26r] armes and his legges drawen out along with cordis &

ropes, & þan his holy & blessid body peynfully ficchid to
þe croys, and cruely was he reryd on hy and agayn þrowen
adoun violently & dispitously to þe erthe, þat alle þe veynes 870
& synwes of hys body were broken & brosten, wherof þe
welle of mercy þat neuere schal cece ne fayle flowed out in
large strem[e]s vn-to synners to wassche and purge hem of
her gyltes. And ȝif, par cas, yt semeth to þe þat his blood
suffiseth nat to clense þe, þanne remembre the of þe pre- 875
cious water that stremyd out from his herte, þat was þerlyd
wiþ a scharp spere, to wassche awey perfitly þe synnes of
contryt folkes.

The insensible creatures (þat is to seyn, the creatures þat
hadde no felynge ne lyf) [h]adden sorwe and heuynesse of 880
his greet and scharp passyon. The Iewes, whoos hertes ben
hardere þan stones, "cnokkydon her brestes" [Luke 23:48],
whan Crist suffryde alle his tormentȝ. [26v] þe sonne wyth-
drow hys bemes, "& derknesses apperden on the erthe"
[Matt. 27:45; Luke 23:44]. "[The veil of the temple was torn 885
atwo; the erthe] quok; the dede man roos vp; and the harde
stones," for thei hadde noon eyen wiþ whiche þe[i] myȝt
caste out teres and sorwes, "weren kut atwo" in þe myddes
in tokne of sorwe and heuynesse of so dispitous, so vniust,
and so merueylos a passion [Matt. 27:51–52; Luke 23:45]. 890
Wherof, God seith be apyn tokne to vs by the prophete:
"Taketh hede," he seyth, "and seeth ȝif þer be any sorwe
lyk to my sorwe" [Lam. 1:12]. O louynge sorwe, O passion
ful of vertues, O necessarie & byhoueful deeth vn-to alle
synneres, wherof wellyd out þe oyle of mercy, þat neuere 895
schal fayle, wherof sprong also the welle of pyte & grace,
and þe medicyn of helþe spradde out largely to alle folk in
þe ryueres of the precious blood of Ihesu Crist, schede for
vs in vijᵉ maner wyses to make satisfaccion and redresse
for the omyssion and leuynge [of] þe vijᵉ werkes of mercy 900
& for þe offense or trespace in þe vijᵉ deedly syn- [27r] nes
as vn-to alle þo þat han wil for to repente and rewe her
wykkydnesse & aske mercy.

Therfore, O þu synnere, often byhalde and see bisili and
deuoutly. First, honoure and worschipe thow þe stremees 905
& þe ryueres þat ron doun fro þe heed of Crist, þat was
coronyd for thi synnes wiþ scharp þornes, by-sechynge hym

in al meknesse þat he do awey al þat þow hast synnyd by
vnleefful vsage of þin heed with þe v wyttes ficchid in it,
and þat þe humble & meke inclinacion or bowynge of          910
Cristes heed in þe croys wiþ-drawe fro the þe synn<e>
of pride.

Secundely, byhoold þe clene blood of Cristes herte, cruely woundyd with a spere, þat he clense and purge þe of al
þat euere þu hast synnyd by vnclene þouȝt and vnliefful     915
wyl, & þat he putte awey fer fro þe þe synne of envie.

The iijᵉ, by-hoold wel þe cours of blood þat cam out of
Crystes handes þat weren cruely þerlyd for þe, þat i[t] may
wasshe awei al [27v] þat þow hast synned by vnliefful werkynge of þine handes, and lat þe nakkydnes of Crist han-    920
gynge in the croys make þe nakyd and baare of coueytous
desir.

The iiijᵉ, byhold thow þe flowynge blood passynge out for
þe in strong stremes of scharp scourges of þe body of Ihesu
Crist, þat it may wassche away al þat þu haast synned by    925
vnleefful vsage of þi body, and þat he asswage & abregge
in the þe prikkynge o[r] þe styrynges of ire or of wratthe,
in-as-moche as he preyde for hem þat ⁺ weren his
to<r>mentoures.

The vᵉ, biholde "þe dropes of þe blody swoot of Crist þat    930
fil doun to þe erthe" for the [Luke 22:44], þat yt may clense
al þat þat þu hast synnyd by þe superflu or outrageous vsage
of temporal goodes, and þat þe honger, the fastynge, & þe
þirst of Crist which weryn fillid by þe bittyrnesse of eysil
and gall, mowe refreyne or withdrawe þin excessyf and      935
vnliefful glotenye.

The viᵉ, byhoold & see the tendre blood [28r] of þe ȝonge
childissch membres of Crist, þat was circumcised for þe viijᵉ
day with a scharp stoon, til þat [it may] al þin vnliefful
concupiscence or fleschly desir dist[r]oye [and] quenche in  940
the þe temptacions of lecherye.

And þe vijᵉ, byhoold and se þe flodes of blood distillynge
& droppynge doun fro þe nayle[d] feet of Crist, which for
thi love for-sook nat ne lothid nat to bere his owen croys
toward the same torment, that he kepe þe fro þe synne of    945
sleuthe and þat he graunte the continuel besynesse in good
& vertuous werkes.

Thus, lo, after þe conseyl of Helyse the prophete:
"Wassch þe vij^e sythes in Iordan, and þi flesch schal receyve
helþe, and þu schalt be clensyd" [4 Kings 5:10]. Now ȝif a        950
man take hertly heede to þese þinges, what synnere may
dispey[r]e or myshope of pardon or forȝeu[en]esse, whiles
in Our Saueour, byhetynge vs his mercy, been concurrent
or knyt togydre his hi myȝt þat may nat be let, his infallable
or vndeceyuable trouthe, and [28v] his <e>ntier dileccion        955
or loue of charite to vs-ward, which is so greet and so excellent þat tonge of man suffiseþ nat to telle yt. In signe or
tokne of which dileccion, the heed of Cryst hanginge in þe
croys ys enclyned or bowed doun to profre vs a kus, his
armes ben out-strecchid to enbrace or clippe vs; þe herte       960
is opnyd wyde to love vs; his handes and feet ben ficchid
to þe croys to duelle with vs perpetuely. Ffor vnto the
worldys ende, Crist schal duelle with vs bodyly in the holy
and blisful sacrament of the autier, where euery-day, vndir
þe figure or liknesse of breed and wyn, hys soule ys offred     965
vn-to vs in-to þe prys of oure redempcion—þe bodi in-to
spirituel mete, þe blood in-to drynke of helþe, and þe watir
of his syde in-to oure lauour [or] clensynge, and al in-to a
noble confortatyf agay[n] the fendes temptacions.

The croys of Crist ys þe verray "[tree of] lyf" [Gen. 2:9],      970
whos excellently vertuous fruyt hath destroyd þe venym
þat sp[r]ang [29r] out or was engendrid of þe deffendid or
forboden tree þoruȝ þe offence of oure firste progenitoures,
Adam & Eve. That blysful sacrament of þe auter nurscheth,
strenthith, and confortiþ euery man & womman þat takyth       975
yt worthily [and] knyttiþ hymself verrayly to hys heed,
Crist, as a membre of hys qwykned wiþ his owen blood.
Wherfore, ȝif þow be honured or maad noble þoruȝ þe
gentylnesse of his body and þu passe so out of þis present
ly[ȝt], nouther helle ne the deuel may holde the, and þer        980
schal no peyne perpetuel turmente the, but þow þat art
bouȝt with the prys of so precious blood schalt be worþi
to haue heuenly ioye, and þu schalt fynaly entre in-to þe
blisse of heuene as a k[yn]sman of þe euerlastynge Kyng
of Heuene.                                                        985

ȝyt, natheles, lest so manye and so large benefices of þe
mercy of God freely profred to þe engendre presumpcion,

negligence, or slouthe, behoold eu*ere* [and anon] þe steerne
ryȝtwysnesse of God, þe sorwe- [29v] ful [necessite of þe]
dep*ar*tynge of þe soule fro þe body, & the vncerteynte of      990
tyme, whan þe malicious feendes schullen feerfully appe*re*
byforn þe, tellynge and schewynge vnto þe alle þe synnes
þat þow hast wrouȝt, for the which þu hast [nat] maad satis-
fac*cion*; *þer* schal nat so moche be forgetyn as þe leeste
"ydyl word" or vnleefful þouȝt [Matt. 12:36]. Than wole      995
þei enforce hem to take w*ith* hem þe wrecchid soule vn-to
helle or to purgatorie, which ys ryȝt peynful, & vnto þe
feerful doom of þe Almyȝty Iuge, whos hy ryȝtwysnesse
may suffr*e* no synne vn-punsched.

Vn-to þat tre*m*lynge or qu<a>kynge Iugement schalt      1000
þow sodeynly be callyd. *þer* schal no respyt been had, ne
noon apeel fro þe Iuge schal *þere* avayle, ne noon excusa-
*cion* of synne schal ben admyttid or receyued, where alle
synnes schullen openly be schewyd—as wel to þe Iuge as
to alle creatures—in-so-mochil þat þe moost p*riue* þouȝtes      1005
schullen also be cnowe, wit- [30r] nessynge a *m*annes owen
conscience þat sore fretiþ and gnawyth wyth-ine hymself.
þ*ere* schal ben askyd of þe a ful streit acounte of alle þe
ȝiftes þat God hath ȝouen the and þat þow hast of hym
receyuyd and taken byforn, and also þu schalt acounte of      1010
eu*ery* moment of the tyme of þi lyf here, how þu hast dispen-
did yt to the hono*ur* of [God], & of euery wykkyd deede,
be yt neu*ere* so smal; eu*ery* man schal acounte also of al
þe goodnes þat he hath left vndoon and myȝte haue doon
yt, fro þe ȝeres of his discre*cion* vn-to þe tyme of hys deeth.      1015
O how ma[n]y forȝeten synnes, how many defautes, how
many negligences schul þanne sodeynly breste out as yt
were in awayt to trouble þi wrecchi[d] soule!

ȝif þow come, as God defende yt, in deedly synne to þe
doom, the [h]y Iuge aboue, þe wrat[h]ful & streyt Iuge, þe      1020
Almyȝti Lord schal agaste þe ful sor*e*, and by-nethforth
schal opyn þe pyt of helle [to] make þe to tremble [30v] and
quake, to swolw the in peynnes vntollerable or vnsuffrable.
Wiþ-ineforth þin owen conscience schal sore frete and
gnavve. Byforn the alle thy synnes schul fere þe, for þei      1025
schullen ben knowen openly to God, to his angeles, and to
alle oþere. Byhynde þe schul tormento*ure*s putte the in huge

dreede wiþ her instrumentes *i*nfernaly or hellely to take þe
in-to torment. On the lyf[t] hand, alle þe feendes and da*m*p-
nyd folk schullen accuse the in comune, þat þu hast nat only     1030
offendid God, but þu hast also encrecyd þe *p*erpetuel peynes
of hem alle; ffor þe sonner þat þe day of doom approcheþ
or neyȝeth and the mo folk þat ben dampnyd, þe more
greuous schal ben hir torment and punschinge. On thi ryȝt
hand, alle þe blessyd ordres of men and ⁺ angeles schullen     1035
accuse the, þat þu, duellynge & contynuynge in deedly
synne, fleddest vn-to dampnac*i*on fro the hoost of Cristen
peple & abreggedist and madist lasse þe co*m*panye of hem |

[against temptation; to the evil example of many, you have
not aided the sufferers in purgatory through works of charity, but through your damnable life, you have delayed the
universal glory of the resurrection, when even the heavenly
bodies, the sun, the moon with the other planets and all the
stars, the earth, the sea, and individual elements will be
changed into a state seven times clearer or more perfect
and thus will be rewarded in eternal peace for the service
that, God willing, they have shown men temporally. And,
therefore, all these things surrounding you have complained
to their own possible limits to you, who have thus delayed
their own happiness. Therefore, not without reasonable
cause, if you come to Judgment with mortal sin, each creature to his Judge will cry out against you: "Redress, most
righteous Judge, not only that injury to you, but also that
injury to all your creatures." Therefore, according to the
counsel of the prophet David so often brought to mind, "see
the works of God; who is terrible in his counsels over the
sons of men" (Ps. 65:5).

O what a terrible sentence, O what horrible punishments,
O what interminable sadness after this clamor will pursue
those most justly condemned to the eternal fire! For according to the wisdom of some saints, at the Day of Judgment all filth, all venomous serpents, and all foul smells
suddenly will descend to the center of the world, so that
there, as it were, in the most appropriate place, the inferno,
they may punish the sinner without end. Nor therefore is it
a wonder if infernal torments are horrible and sharp, when

the torments of purgatory, according to the blessed Augustine, are "harder than any of the torments able to be seen or imagined in this life." The inextinguishable fire, the immortal worm, the insatiable thirst, the horrible appearance of demons, the palpable shadows, the intolerable odor, the sudden change from the greatest cold to the greatest heat, the absence of the divine vision and any joy, the great sadness of the heart and the despair of any remedy or aid— all will torment without end the wretched ones in the inferno. For, as I will briefly conclude, there will be nothing delightful in that place, no consolation, no comfort, but everything will be there that is able to punish or harm, and this irremediably without end. O therefore wretched soul, according to the counsel of the prophet Jeremiah, more frequently see "that it is an evil and a bitter thing for thee, to have left the Lord thy God and that [his] fear is not with thee" (Jer. 2:19). Thus, likewise, you recluses, through necessary timely meditation, "see your vocation" (1 Cor. 1:26).]

# [Part 3: Practicing the Contemplative Life

## CHAPTER 1: RECOMMENDATIONS ON PRAYER]

[Thirdly, you will see in this work, you recluses, how you will practice your calling, for as it is shown above, you are called to perpetual prayer, meditation, reading, or some honest manual labor. Therefore, through consideration of your assets or defects in those matters, see how you have performed your vocation.

First, concerning required or customary prayers, each night before you may allow yourself to sleep, you may mentally make a faithful reckoning to yourselves of how much service to God has been offered that day. If you have fulfilled your habitual duty fully, devotedly, without distraction of mind, with compunction of heart or some sweetness of holy tears, you may render sincere thanks to God, attributing all goodness in your works to his grace and mercy, not to your virtues. However, if you perform the divine service inadequately, lukewarmly, with distraction of the mind on vain, vile, or useless things, or without the warmth or sweetness of devotion, what is lacking may be immediately absolved; for the remnants of fault, your breast may repeatedly be struck, sincere sighs may be provoked; by virtue of the tenderness toward avowed feelings, "the bowels of the mercy of our God" [Luke 1:78] may be affected, and you, on such a day, may reckon yourselves to have been evil servants, "unprofitable" and unworthy (Luke 17:10).

Here it is profitable to understand how terrifyingly Holy Scripture speaks of these who are in some manner deficient in performing God's service. For concerning those speaking inadequately, it is written in Jeremiah: "Cursed be he that doth the work of the Lord deceitfully" (Jer. 48:10). Concerning those lukewarm in speaking, who are neither completely frigid through lack of devotion and apparent mortal sin, nor ardent or hot through the fervor of devotion, but as it were, are sluggish by sloth and idleness, it is said in Apocalypse: "I would thou wert cold, or hot. But because thou art luke-warm, . . . I will begin to vomit thee out of my mouth" (Apoc. 3:15–16). And of those distracted in prayer, through vain and illicit thoughts, the Lord indignantly says: "This people . . . with their lips glorify me, but their heart is far from me" (Isa. 29:13).

Against such manifold wanderings of the mind in prayer, there might sometimes be a remedy: if a prayer is read aloud from a book accompanied by prayers not required but vol-untary, and at the same time anyone is distracted in vocal prayer, immediately, for a remedy, let the prayer be silent. If even in this way the tempter may not fail to disquiet, in the future may be requested the most noble]

[31r] medicyn for euery temptacion, and þat is þe herty biholdynge and remembraunce of Cristes passyon in the   1040 croys, which—of the excellent love þat he hadde vn-to þe, to make satisfaccion and amendys for thy synnes and to ʒeve þe myʒti vertu of resistence or wiþstondynge agayn alle temptacions—baar a crowne of þorn on his heed, which stak scharply and soore vn-to þe touchynge or þirlynge of   1045 [þe] brayn, and on euery part droppyd doun precious droopes of blood vn-to þe medycyn and heele of þe. Also, he profreed frely to þe the love of his herte, whan blood and water flowed out of yt þat was cruely woundid wiþ a spere to hele þe hurtes & woundes of synful folk. Moore-   1050 [o]uyr, his handis and his feet were faste ficchid to þe croys wyth harde nayles of yren, for to duelle and abyde wyth þe in temptacions, and þei schedden out lycour in greet abundaunce or plente to þe perfyt medycyn of euery spiry-
[31v] tual hurt or syknesse þat man may have. Vn-to þat   1055 medycyn clepith vs and byddiþ vs to come þe scripture, þat seyth þus: "Seeth þe Kyng Salomon wyth þe dyademe wiþ þe which his modir coronyd hym" [Song Sol. 3:11]. And in an-oþir place seyth Crist in þis wyse: "Whi or wher-to be ʒe troublyd, and whi ascenden þouʒtes in-to ʒoure hertes?   1060 Byholdeth myn handes and my feet" [Luke 24:38–39].

O a hool-sum syȝte, O a suffisaunt medycyn of helþe, O
precious passion figuryd or lyknyd by þe serpent of bras,
þat perfitly heelest alle þo þat be smeten or hurt of þe fyry
serpentes of temptacion, whan men hertly byholden þe,        1065
askynge þin help and confort! Whan þu art distract or temptyd, bihold often þis passion; here seek þi socour; here aske;
here knowe; go nat awey; stinte nat, til þow have receyuyd
sum medycyn, seyinge feiþfully to Oure Lord wiþ [þe] prophete, "Lord, 'purge or clense [me] of myn hid synnes'"    1070
[Ps. 18:13]. Also, "Hele me, Lord, and I [32r] schal ben
helyd; make me saaf and I schal be sauyd" [Jer. 17:14]. Lo
now, Lord, I, wrecche and beggere, nedy and vnworthi,
come vnto the welle of þi mercy, þat schal neuere fayle, and
vn-to þe infynyt & plenteuously heepyd grace, which þu    1075
hast disposyd & ordeynyd wyth-outen ende and haast
mercyablely beheyght to deele and departe it liberaly and
freely to wrecchyd synneres and to hem þat ben temptyd.
þerfore schal I feythfully seeke; I schal aske; I schal knowe;
and I schal crye lamentably or sorwefully tyl I be confortid   1080
in sum wyse. I woot wel, mercyable Lord, þu wylt nat putte
awey þe wrecche þat beggeth mekly. I byleve, benygne
"wardeyn and kepere of men" [Job 7:20], þat þu schalt nat
wyttyrly schitte the lappe or bo[o]sum of thi grace fro hym
that verrayly & mekly askyth þi mercy. And þouȝ I haue    1085
deseruyd no mercy, ȝit naþeles, þoruȝ þi souereyn bounte,
ȝif me a lytyl of þin abundance of þin hy pite, for a ful smal
thing may feede & [32v] refressche me, synful wrecche. Al-
þouȝ I be vnworthi, ȝit graunte, natheles, to myn indigence
sum lytil paart or sum droope of thi precious & holy blood    1090
þat my scharp herte may be onyd or knyt to þe by love
wyth-oute dissolucion or disseuerance, and þat al distractynge or a-stonynge of þouȝt may þe sonnere vansche
away fro me. And ȝif I may nat haue of the blood of þin
herte or of þin heed or of þin handes, I byseche þe humblely,    1095
mercyful Lord, ȝeue & dele to me, þat preie vn-to þe &
begge of þe, be yt neuere so lytil, of þe blody floodes of ⁺
þi blessed feet, for douteles I am ful nedy; I seke to þe, I
aske of þe, I knokke at þe ȝate of þi mercy, & certeyn
[am] nat wyllynge to departe with-oute receyuynge of þin    1100
confortable helpynge. I woot wel, Lord, I woot wel þat þouȝ

þu ӡeue or graunte me neuere so lytil of þi precious blood,
it is of suych force & suych vertu þat nat only suffiseth to
the he[lth]e of me, but also to al þe worldes helthe, & it is
i-nowӡ, plen- [33r] te to refreyne, to chace, to agaste, and     1105
to ouyrcome al þe power or myӡt of þe feend.

The besy instance of suych a preiere, þoruӡ þe grace of
Almӡti God, schal opteene and haue þe victorie. And ӡif
in spiritual batayle a-gayn temptacions or vnleefful
þouӡtes, any man be + maad weery or be troublyd þoruӡ      1110
trauayle and dreede, heuynesse or sorwe, so he nat fully
assente to any deedly synne, al þat exercise ys merytorie
& meedful +; al hepith & gadreþ meryt to-gidre; al [is] occasion or cause o[f] [m]eede; al purueyeth and al ordeyneth
corones of glorie in tyme comynge.                               1115

Now, þoruӡ þe mediacion of Goddes grace and by posses-
sion or hauynge of hertes quie<t>t & reste, it is to considere þat nòþing be askyd in preyere þat is contrarie to þe
wyl of God, no superflu or outrageous þinges (þat is to
seyn, ovir-mochil or out of mesure); aske nothing but yt be      1120
necessarie to þe helþe of body or of soule, nothing þat is
contrarie to charite. Out of [33v] charite schal procede or[i]-
son & preiere and strecche as wiel to enemys as freendes,
alþouӡ by-tuexe whiles a man may preie more specialy for
hym-self and for hem þat he ys moost bonden or holden to.       1125
The charite of hym þat preyeth schal beholde and se the
needes of pore folk [and] pilgrymes, passyons and diseses
of feeble & syke folk, the chargeable besyness of princes
and prelates, the myseries & wrecchidnesses of outlawed
folk and of hem þat bien in prison, the greete laboures of      1130
werkmen & of hem þat trauayle, + þe dreedes & perilles of
schipmen and of laboureres, &—schortly to speke to—þe
temptacions and anguissches and tribulacions of alle men.
For alle þese þinges, + recluses schal often calle & knokke
on mercyable God, wiþ sorweful teres & þoruӡ sighynges        1135
prouoke and stire God to do mercy, grace, & socour. And
þis is an holy þing; þis is a swete and plesaunt þing to God;
& this ys "a clene oblacion & offrynge" [Mal. 1:11]; þis ys
an accep[table] |

[offering to God, the most useful and profitable to whoever
does this for his neighbors. So, therefore, you recluses,

through watchful consideration of your prayer, "see your vocation" (1 Cor. 1:26).]

# [CHAPTER 2: RECOMMENDATIONS ON MEDITATION]

[Secondly, concerning your devout meditations, each night you may reckon how much you have advanced and how much you have failed that day. For any progress, you may give thanks to God, and for any failure, you may sincerely suffer pain. Then true meditation advances, when it inspires the fear of God in sinners, inflames his love in the lukewarm and the undevout, provokes tears of devotion, multiplies the praises of God, generates hatred of sin, and increases the desire for an honest life, and even fixes the mind on heavenly things. Whence concerning the contemplative man the prophet says that "He shall sit solitary and hold his peace" and raise himself above himself (Lam. 3:28). In meditations of this kind, many have advanced, because many have some foretaste of the sweetness of future blessedness in the delectation of divine goodness and his high beauty, in the revelation of future things, in the conversation of the angels, but also in some sort of vision and ineffable consolation of the Almighty Himself. Likewise, the prophet David says, "O taste and see that the Lord is sweet" (Ps. 33:9).

O gracious taste, O precious vision, O sweetness above all beloved delights of the world! While truly to the solitary contemplative the burning love of God becomes sweet, every worldly joy assuredly withers. To whom cinnamon is delicious and redolent, vile lye is not pleasing. Whom the most beloved flower and fruit delight, the deformed stalk does not comfort, and to whom the spring]

[34r] of swetnesse sauoureþ & floweþ out habundauntly, alle    1140
oþer3 lycoures leefen hir sauour þat first hadden good taast.
Ryȝt so, sooþly, who-so þat taasteþ þe delyces of paradys
(þat is to seyn, þe swetnesse of þe brennynge love of God),
he settiþ at nauȝt alle manere of worldly lustes, as some

þat weren expert & knowynge in þis caas lefte wryten &     1145
tolde to her famylier foolk. Of suych þe prophete Dauyd
seiþ vn-to Oure Lord þus: "Lord," he seyth, "'þey schul
telle out or expresse the [mynde of] þe abundaunce of thi
swetnesse'" [Ps. 144:7].

But of alle þese þinges whiles we lyuen here, to þinges     1150
ben gretly to dreede, for þe which a circumspect prudence
(þat is to seyn, a wys syȝte, seynge byfore & behynde) is
necessarie, wiþ byhoueful or covenable remedie. On ys, lest
"the angel of Sathenas, transfygurynge hym in-to þe angel
of lyȝt" [2 Cor. 11:14], sotylly ⁺ deceyve & leede folk into     1155
errour; agayn the peril of wham in al his apperynge, ar ȝe
ȝeve any credence or [34v] feyth vn-to hym, maketh a deuout and hertly preyere to God, þat he kepe and defende
contynuely þin ignoraunce & vncunnynge of his seruaunt
fro þe fallaces & deceytes of þe feend. And it is good to     1160
remembre and haue in mynde þat, after þe sentence of
seyntes, þe good angel þat apperyth to men comunely im-
presseþ dreede in a man in þe bygynnynge & confortith hym
aftyrward, but al anoþer dooþ þe wykkyd spiryt, for in his
apperynge he fyrst comforteþ, and aftirward he induceþ or     1165
bryngyth in errour.

An-oþir þyng ys also to dreede in this matere: þat ys to
seyn, lest þe gretnesse of reuelacion or sum oþir gracious
ȝefte or schewynge of God swelle or bolne so greetly in a
man þat he sette ovir-mochil by hymself. Agayn þat peryl     1170
þe verray humilite of þe herte ys to been had and holden
by remembraunce of alle þinges, as wyel of his owen defautes as of þe ȝeftes of God, and þat he holde hym-self
vnworthi and crye and seye wyth [þe] apostil [35r] in this
manere: "By the grace of God, I am þat I am" [1 Cor. 15:10].     1175
And for þat "euery good ȝefte & euery perfyt ȝefte from
above ys descendynge from þe Fadir of lyȝt" [Jas. 1:17],
for alle benefices sey þus: "I ȝelde þonkynges to God" [1
Cor. 1:4, 14]; "Glorie & ioye be to God on hy" [Luke 2:14];
and "Lord, nat to vs, nat to vs, but ȝif þow glorie to thi     1180
naame" [Ps. 113:9] of alle oure good werkes. Thus, lat alwey
þe humylite of herte be kept, which is, after Seynt Austyn,
"an euydent or open signe of Goddys chosen folk." And no
meruayl, for "God ȝeueth al-only grace to humble or meke

folk*es*" [1 Pet. 5:5], "and glorie schal exalte or ryse vp hy*m*    1185
þat is hu*m*ble of spiryt" [Prov. 29:23], as wytnesseth Holy
Wryt.

More-ovir, yt is to knowe þat ryȝth as of alle creatures,
of alle holy wryty*nges,* and of alle þe werk*es* of Cryst may
be drawen out a deuout meditac*i*on and expedyent, ȝyf any    1190
good, profitable, or honest þing be founde in hem, lat yt be
reducyd vnto þe edificac*i*on and pr*o*fyt of vs, and lat yt
finaly be referryd to the l[ov]e, p*r*eisynge, glorie, & hono*ur*
of God, for the moost plente- [35v] vous fruyt of our*e* lawe
standiþ p*r*incipaly in the love of God, aftir the wordes of þe    1195
apostel, þat seith þus: "The f[u]lnesse or abundaunce of
lawe ys loue" [Rom. 13:10]. Thus happyth or falleþ a defaute
in þese þinges, ȝif þe þouȝt be rauysschid or ȝeuen to
veyn or vnliefful þinges, ȝif þat þe wil or delectac*i*on þat a
man hath [ben] in any cr*e*ature finaly, or ȝif þe vndirstan-    1200
dynge or reson inwardly erre in the feyth of Holy Cherche or
in þe Artycles of the Feyth det*er*mynyd by Holy Cherche.

Of dystractynge of þouȝt and of a creture þat ys nat for
to be louyd but finaly for God, to þo twey materes ben
seyd above sufficiently. But for the erro*ur* þat may be of    1205
vndirstondynge, it profite[t]h þat þe Articles of þe Feyth,
þat ben conteyned in the Byleve of þe Apostles and in þe
Byleve of Athanasie, be fully vndirstonden, bele[eu]ed
stedefastly, and taken vn-to memorie or mynde, and þat
nothing þat longiþ to þe feyth [+] be disputyd ne be [36r]    1210
othir-wise beleeuyd þan was byforn, w*ith*oute conseyl of a
wys devyn, but eu*er*y man knytte hym stedefastly & myȝtyly, wiþ-oute hesitac*i*on or doute, to þ[e] byleve of oure
modyr of Holy Cherche, þouȝ he haue nat in some articles
euydence or tokne of reson, ffor after þe wordes of Seynt    1215
Gregory, "Ffeyth hath no meryt, wher*e* ma*n*nes reson
ȝeueth experyment or preef."

To materes namly þ*er* be of oure lawe þat passen ful feer
the intelligence or reson of eu*er*y man: þat ys to sey, þat þe
Fadir & Sone and Holy Goost ben þre p*er*sones distynct, of    1220
þe wyche noon ys other*es* p*er*sone, and ȝyt nathelees þo
þre p*er*sones ben substancialy oon & þe same God; and
also, þat þe myddyl p*er*sone, which ys þe Sone of God wiþ-
outen bygynnynge or endynge, by þe op*er*acion and wer-

kynge of þe Holy Goost, sodeynly whan hys wyl was or    1225
whan he wolde, took his body of the clennest blody dropes
of þe Blessid Virgine for oure helþe, þat so þe same Sone
of God, which was [36v] maad man, in his deedes and doc-
trines scholde ȝeue vs a forme of perfyt lyf, and at þe laste,
for the satisfaccion of oure synne, he suffrid harde deeþ in    1230
oure nature þat he took [and] left wiþ vs hys body & hys
blood vndyr lyknesse of breed & wyn in-to perpetuel
nurschynge, remedie, and solace spirituel. This blessyd sacrament vndir suych lyknesse disposyd & ordeyned Almyȝty God, which ben moost conuenyent to þe nurschynge    1235
of man, leest d[r]eede or wlatsomnesse of a raw body or
blood scholde wiþdrawe Cristen folk fro þe communyon or
receyuynge of þat precious body, and for þat stedefast byleve scholde many-foold more encrece his meryt agayn þe
experience o[r] þe vndirstondynge of his owen wyt. ȝe    1240
schulle stedefastly byleve þat, þouȝ—be þe vertu of þe
wordes sacramental, þat Crist ordeynyd and þe preest hys
viker seyth—oonly vndir þe lyknesse of breed ys þe flessch
of Cryst and [37r] vndir þe lyknesse of wyn oonly ys blood,
ȝet be þe consecracion naþeles for þat of þe wyl of God,    1245
the blood schal nat be deseuered ne departid fro þe flessch,
ne soule fro þe body, ne þe manhode fro þe deite of
Godhede; þerfor, vndir eyther lyknesse (þat ys to seyn, as
wiel of breed as wyn), whan þe consecracion is maad, yt ys
flessch & blood, body, soule, and þat same Godhede, al    1250
Crist, verray God and man.

Ther ben some similitudes in nature [þat] mowe, as in
manere, induce a man and make hym þe moore strong in
the feyth. As thus, wheþir breed and wyn dygest or diffyed
in a litil tyme in þe stomak of man þorugh naturel heete    1255
been turnyd in-to verray flessch & verray blood of þe etere
and drynkere? ȝys. Where-fore, may nat God Almyȝti,
maker of al þinges, þat maade al þis world of nauȝt only
wyth woord, turne sodey[n]ly breed and wyn in-to hys
flessch and blood þoruȝ þe vertu of þe wordes? Ne lat yt    1260
stire no man, ne make hym flecche or varie fro [37v] + þe
ryȝt byleeue þat in euen wyse aftir þe consecracion duellen
as þer diden biforn accidentes (þat is to sey, colour, sauour,
and weyghte) of breed and wyn whan þer is neyþer þere

breed, ne wyn, ne noon oþir substance but substance of þe   1265
body and of þe blood of Ihesu Crist wiþ the Godhede. And
þat is no wonder whiles, as seith þe philesofre aftir þe oold
translacion, þat o metal, as coper, may be robbyd of his
owen accidentes and be cloþed wiþ accidentes o[f] syluyr
or gold, þat it may seeme syluyr or gold in weyghte & col-   1270
our. Ryʒt so, ʒif þe hoost consecrat be departid, let no
man doute but þat hoolly & fully þe body & þe blood of
Crist perseuereth and duelleth vndir euery part of þe dyuy-
sion or departynge, as yt falleth or happeth naturaly in a
broken myrour, in euery broken part of þe whiche þe same   1275
ymage schyneth and schewyth as yt dide fyrst in the hool
myrrour.

More-ovir, euery Cristen man schal stydefastly byleve þat
in [þe] same manere as wel þe body of Crist as [h]ys blood,
which he took of þe Blessyd Virgine and in |                  1280

[which he suffered on the cross for us, truly is in every
consecrated host. Nor is this difficult for God, who makes
it possible that the same speaker's voice might be multiplied
naturally for the individual ears of the hearers.

Moreover, it must be believed that any particle of the host
will be able to contain the body of Christ, which first
emerged from the closed womb of the Virgin and later, "the
doors being shut" (John 20:26), came to the disciples.

Hereupon, through faith, "stand and see the great won-
ders" of the Lord (Exod. 14:13), as Moses urged the people.
For all these things ought to be believed by firm faith, chiefly
because of the authority of the ineffable truth, which says,
"I am the bread of life" (John 6:35), and "If any man eat of
this bread, he shall live for ever; and the bread that I will
give, is my flesh, for the life of the world" (John 6:52). "For
my flesh," he says, "is meat indeed: and my blood is drink
indeed" (John 6:56).

O most precious nourishment, O most noble restorative,
O most efficacious comfort, in which is concealed for the
cleansed souls "all that is delicious" and the spiritual sweetness "of every taste" (Wisd. 16:20)! Why, O wretched soul,
do you ask solace, aid, or succor elsewhere? Elsewhere are
the creatures; here is the Omnipotent Creator. Elsewhere

are the relics of the saints; here is the founder, king, and lord of all the Saints. No others are able to do anything unless through his strength. Others are not to be loved or honored except for his love, praise, glory, and honor. Each day this God and Lord of all offers himself freely to you, so that you may show your need, ask for mercy, plead for grace, and receive whatever might be necessary to you for your salvation. Therefore, fear not a shortage in necessary things, nor may you tremble in difficulties and tribulations, nor may you despair in any temptations, because the Father of Mercy always concedes to the supplicant whatever he humbly asks or whatever is better for the petitioner.

You recluses, you ought to employ firm faith in all these things, and thus, through the habit of blessed meditation, "see your vocation" (1 Cor. 1:26).]

# Emendations

| | |
|---|---|
| 1 | messager] sager. |
| 10 | hyle] hyld. |
| 38–39 | decernyd] deceyuyd. |
| 39 | therfor] therfor of. |
| 43 | plenteuously] pleteuously. |
| 53 | occupacions] *macron om.* |
| 58 | fro] for. |
| 73 | þe] þei. |
| 109 | cloþis] cloþid. |
| 113 | nat] *om.* |
| 127–28 | vertuous] *vertuos.* |
| 136 | But] be. |
| 138 | entendynge] entedynge. |
| 140 | ne] ney. |
| 142 | accustumed] accusmed. |
| 147 | erþe] *om.* |
| 154 | forþan] lord þan. |
| 167 | ryȝtwys] rytȝtwys. |
| 173 | who] ho. |
| 175 | ofte-tymes] ofte-tymes that. |
| 208 | hym (1)] *om.* |
| 215 | God] good. |
| 224 | with] *supralinear* owt *follows.* |
| 225 | ende +, on] endes of. |
| 229 | I byseche] *repeated.* |
| 246 | purueyance] purueynce. |
| 266 | þei] þa. |
| 277 | schewed] *followed by* doon *crossed through in red.* |
| 316 | to] *repeated.* |
| 318 | or] of. |
| 320 | hadde] *repeated.* |
| 325 | hoolsum] hoosum *followed by gap in line.* |
| 328 | be] *om.* |
| 340 | or] *om.* |
| 351–52 | feruentnesse] feruenese *with the* ne *a supralinear addition.* |

353   Call] I callyd.
362   Dalida] dalyaunce.
387   or] of.
394   hym] hem.
397   enclosed] *repeated.*
397   her (2)] he.
406   per-caas] per-caas þat.
408   & ȝif þei ben] *om.*
408   &] (2) *om.*
409   engendringe] engendringe *with.*
413   or] of.
419   storie] storie þat.
439   fleschly] c *over a long stroke.*
445–46   deemyd] deemmyd.
451   continuel] continiel.
454   presynge] plesynge.
456   soote] softe.
463   greetly] geetly.
487–88   studyinge] studynge.
494   greuyth] greuyt.
497   it] *om.*
498   hem] hey.
500   schewyd] schewy.
503   in (1)] i.
504   open] opey.
508   in] *om.*
510   spyrituel] spytuel.
533   merveylous] merveylous þe.
543   on] or *with macron over the* o.
544   þat] *repeated.*
563   of] to.
568   of] *om.*
574   entent] *extra minim with first* n.
575   al þe] *repeated.*
580   nat (1)] *om.*
583   which is] wiþ his.
588   þerin, þouȝ] þe inþouȝt.
605   remeyneth] *extra minim with* n.
619   disposicions] disposicion.
644   fect] feet.
646   þouȝ]  þoruȝ.
653   þis] þan.
665   wiþ] which.

667 þys] y *over indistinguishable letter.*
675 effectual] effectualy.
678 forȝeuenesse]   forȝeuesse.
681–82 forȝeuenesse]   forȝeuesse.
695 þoruȝh] h *over* t.
708 ys] *om.*
711 God] God he.
726–27 necessarie sustenance] necessarienance.
728 wiþ] *om.*
733 Alþouȝ]   also þoruȝ.
733 of] as.
734–35 it . . . at] folwyth by þat preiere þat is moore profitable to.
745 ȝoure]   þoure.
746 distractinge] distringe.
749 Goddys] gooddys.
752 of (1)] *om.*
757 ȝow]  *om.*
778 is] *om.*
779 Holy . . . the] *om.*
782 vndirstondynge] vndirstonde.
792 þe] þi.
796 or (1)] of.
801 sterynge] *three minims for* n.
804 Wheþir] wher.
811 alle] *om.*
814 ȝis] þis.
823 to] *om.*
832 fro] for.
848 tristy] þersty.
860 scornfuly] scornful þat.
865 þorlede] þolede.
873 stremes] stremees.
880 hadden] ladden.
885–86 The . . . erthe] *om.*
887 þei] þe.
900 of (1)] for.
911 synne] *inkblot obscures* e *over* d.
918 it] i.
927 or (1)] *om.*
928 þat] þat he.
929 tormentoures] *first* r *obscured by inkblot.*
939 it may] *om.*
940 and] or.

943 nayled] nayles.
952 dispeyre] dispeyse.
952 forȝeuenesse] forȝeuesse.
955 entier] *first* e *over* t.
968 or] of.
969 agayn] agay.
970 tree of] *om.*
972 sprang] spang.
976 and] *om.*
980 lyȝt] lyf.
984 kynsman] knysman.
988 and anon] among.
989 necessite of þe] *om.*
993 nat] *om.*
1000 quakynge] *capital* a *over illegible letter.*
1012 God] good.
1016 many (1)] may.
1018 wrecchid] wrecchil.
1020 hy] by.
1020 wrathful] wratful.
1022 to] *om.*
1029 lyft] lyf.
1035 and] *repeated.*
1046 þe] þi.
1050–51 Moore-ouyr] moore euyr.
1069 þe] *om.*
1070 me] *om.*
1084 boosum] bot sum.
1097 of (3)] *repeated with* o *crossed through.*
1100 am] *om.*
1104 helthe (1)] herte.
1110 man be] *repeated.*
1113 & meedful] *repeated.*
1113 is] his.
1114 of meede] or neede.
1117 quiett] *inkblot distorts first* t.
1122–23 orison] orson.
1127 and (1)] *om.*
1131 trauayle] trauayle in.
1134 þinges] þinges &.
1148 mynde of] *om.*
1155 sotylly] sotylly to.
1174 þe] *om.*

1193    love] lawe.
1196    fulnesse] foulnesse.
1200    ben] *om.*
1206    profiteth] profiteh.
1208    beleeued] beleueed.
1210    feyth] feyth to.
1213    þe] þi.
1231    and] *om.*
1236    dreede] deede.
1240    or] of.
1252    þat] *om.*
1259    sodeynly] sodeyly.
1261    fro] *repeated.*
1269    of] or.
1279    þe (1)] *om.*
1279    hys] ys.

# Textual and Explanatory Notes

The following abbreviations are used in the notes:

MED   *Middle English Dictionary.* 1954-.
OED   *Oxford English Dictionary.* 2d ed. 1989.
PL    *Patrologiae Cursus Completus. Series Latina.* Ed. J.-P. Migne. 221 vols. Paris, 1844–1903.

10   "hyl[e] and pour*e* out on vs": The scribe apparently misreads a final, broken-circle *e* as *d*, producing "hyld" for "hyle" [*MED hilen* v. 1.(a) To cover (sth.), spread over]. Ln. "Effunde . . . super nos."

10–11   "thin oyle of thi m*e*rcy . . . the welle of thi pite and of thi grace": Cf. "þe welle of m*e*rcy" (871–72); "wellyd out þe oyle of m*e*rcy" (895); "the welle of pyte & grace" (896); and "welle of þi m*e*rcy" (1074). Elsewhere, the formula is applied to Mary (see Marta Powell Harley, *A Revelation of Purgatory by an Unknown, Fifteenth-Century Woman Visionary: Introduction, Critical Text, and Translation,* Studies in Women and Religion, no. 18 [New York: Edwin Mellen Press, 1985], 77, 107 n. 599).

15   "wheþre": The translator makes frequent use of this mark of interrogation preceding a direct question [*OED whether* II. *conj.*]. Here and at lines 66 and 154, it translates Ln. "Numquid" (elsewhere Ln. "Nonne").

22   "on-tendynge": 'paying attention, giving heed, devoting one-self' [*MED entenden* v. 2.(a)]. Ln. "vacandi."

26   "sleuthi folk": 'slothful people' [*MED sleuthi* adj.]. Ln. "accidiososis."

29   "Tayse": Like St. Mary of Egypt, mentioned in lines 29–30, Thais (4th c.?) is celebrated as a converted prostitute. According to the legend, Thais was enclosed for three years in a cell before her acceptance into conventual life. For early accounts of the life of Thais, see *De Vitis Patrum, Liber Primus,* "Vita S. Thaisis, Meretricis" (*PL* 73:661–64); and

48

Jacobus de Voragine, *The Golden Legend of Master William Caxton Done Anew,* 3 vols. (London, 1892), 3:908–10. For modern summaries, see Benedictine Monks of St. Augustine's Abbey, comps., *The Book of Saints: A Dictionary of Servants of God Canonized by the Catholic Church,* 6th ed. (London: A & C Black, 1989), 532; and *The Catholic Encyclopedia,* 1907 ed., s.v. "Thais."

29–30 "Marie Egypcian": Like Thais, St. Mary of Egypt (5th c.?) was an Alexandrian prostitute. Following her dramatic conversion at the Holy Sepulchre in Jerusalem, she lived a penitential life in the desert. Early accounts include *De Vitis Patrum, Liber Primus,* "Vita Sanctae Mariae Ægyptiacae, Meretricis" (*PL* 73:671–90); Jacobus de Voragine, *Golden Legend,* 1:440–43; *The Early South-English Legendary,* ed. Carl Horstmann, Early English Text Society, o.s., 87 (1887; reprint, Millwood, NY: Kraus, 1973), 260–71; and *The South English Legendary, Volume 1,* ed. C. D'Evelyn and A. J. Mill, Early English Text Society, o.s., 235 (London: Oxford Univ. Press, 1959), 136–48. For modern summaries, see Benedictine Monks, *Book of Saints,* 379, and *The Catholic Encyclopedia,* 1907 ed, s.v. "Mary of Egypt." In Chaucer's Man of Law's Tale, Constance's survival at sea elicits the lawyer's rhetorical question, "Who fedde the Egipcien Marie in the cave, / Or in desert?" (Geoffrey Chaucer, *The Riverside Chaucer,* ed. Larry D. Benson, 3d ed. [Boston: Houghton Mifflin, 1987], 94.500–501).

32 "Paule, the firste heremyte": St. Paul the Hermit (c. 230–342) reputedly spent ninety years in the Theban desert, where he lived alone in mountain caves. See Jerome, *Vita S. Pauli* (*PL* 23:17–28); Jacobus de Voragine, *Golden Legend,* 1:318–21. For modern synopses, see Benedictine Monks, *Book of Saints,* 434, and *The Catholic Encyclopedia,* 1907 ed., s.v. "Paul the Hermit."

32 "Hyllarion": St. Hilarion (c. 291–371) is credited with introducing the solitary life in Gaza. See Jerome, *Vita S. Hilarionis* (*PL* 23:29–54). Modern summaries are found in Benedictine Monks, *Book of Saints,* 269–70, and *The Catholic Encyclopedia,* 1907 ed., s.v. "Hilarion."

34–36 "as was in wyldirnesse aftir þe Ascencion of Oure Lord, Marie Maudeleyne, which 'chees þe beste paart'": The reference shows the traditional Western conflation of Mary Magdalene (the apostle) and Mary of Bethany (sister of Martha and Lazarus). See n682 below. Mary Magdalene's legendary pursuit of the contemplative life is recounted in Jacobus de Voragine, *Golden Legend,* 2:619–30: "In this mene whyle the blessyd marie magdalene, desyrous of souerayn contemplacion, sought a ryght sharp deserte, & toke a place whiche was ordeyned by thangele of god, and abode there by the space of xxx yere without knowleche of ony body. In whiche place she had no comfort of rennyng water, no solace of trees, ne of herbes. And that was bycause our redemer dyd do shewe it openly, that he had ordeyned for her refection celestial, and no bodily metes. And euery day at euery hour canonycal she was lift vp in thayer of thangellis, and herd the gloryous song of the heuenly companyes with her bodily eeres. Of whiche she was fedde and fylled with right swete metes, and thenne was brought agayn by thangellis vnto her propre place, in such wyse as she had no nede of corporal norisshyng" (2:626). See also *Early South-English Legendary,* 462–80 (esp. lines 539–641); and *South English Legendary* 302–15 (esp. lines 275–348).

38–39 "dece[rn]yd": 'understood' [*MED discernen* v. 3.(a)]. Ln. "discerni." In writing "deceyuyd," the scribe has mistaken long *r* and *n* for *yu.*

58 "children of perdicion": Cf. John 17:12, 2 Thess. 2:3.

60 "scripule or wem of conscience": 'pang or defect of conscience' [*MED scrupul* n. (c); *OED wem* sb. 2.]. Ln. "consciencie scrupulo."

61 "byscopes nullatenses": 'bogus bishops, Bishops of Nowhere' [*MED Nullatense* n.]. Ln. "episcopi nullatenses." On the emergence of "capellani pontifici o vescovi titolari" in the fourteenth century, see Oliger, "Speculum Inclusorum," 37–40.

63 "lappyd & inuoluyd": 'wrapped and encumbered' [*MED lappen* v. 2a.(a); *involven* v. 1.(a)]. Ln. "involvi."

77 "swychoon": For other instances of the phrase "such a one" as one word, see *OED such* B.V.28.a.

99 "hauntynge": 'practice' [*MED haunting* ger. 2.(a)]. Ln. "frequencia."

100–1 "defoulyd & apeyred": 'defiled and harmed' [*MED defoulen* v. 3.; *apeiren* v. 1.]. Ln. "contaminari et . . . peiorari."

118 The metaphor of spiritual battle or knighthood recurs at lines 182–83, 185–86, 194–96, 312–13, 430–32, and 1109. Cf. 2 Tim. 2:3 and 4:7–8; 2 Cor. 10:3–4; and Eph. 6:10–17. See Evans, "Illustrated Fragment," 17, 30.

124–25 "wiþholde meyne passynge to seruauntȝ": 'retain a household staff greater than two servants' [*OED withhold* v. 4.b.; *MED meine* n. 1.(a)(c)]. Ln. "familiam retinere." See Aelred, *De Institutione,* 3.107–16.

125–26 "bringe forth ȝoong folk custummably, as in multitude or for hyre": 'regularly bring up children in a group or for payment' [*MED custumabli* adv. (a); *hir(e* n. 1.(a)]. Ln. "iuvenes educare." See Aelred, *De Institutione,* 3.116–18.

127–34 "But . . . bothe": These lines represent an expansion of the Latin text.

136–38 "B[ut] . . . apostil": Cf. 1 Tim. 6:8.

140 "disturble or lette": 'impede' [*MED distourblen* v. 2.(a)]. Ln. "inpediat."

152–53 "to plesaunce and lykynge of her God": Cf. Eph. 1:9, 5:10.

174–80 On Satan's transfiguration as the angel of light, see also lines 1153–66, as well as the warnings in Rolle, "Form of Living," 90.51–93.104. The epithets "'þe angel Sathenas'" (175) and "'the angel of Sathenas'" (1154) evidently draw on 2 Cor. 12:7.

178 "heyg": 'high' [*MED heigh* adj.]. The closest spelling in the *MED* entry is *heg(e;* the *OED* records *heygh* and *heyȝ.* The phrase "excitynge hym to entre in-to þat heyg charge" is not found in the Latin.

182–96 On the metahpor of spiritual battle, see n118 above.

188–89 "erþely thinges": Cf. John 3:12, Phil. 3:19.

199 *"thousand":* This expands the manuscript's abbreviation "M¹" for Ln. "Mille."

201–2 "nouþer wole I conseil hym to take it on hyur, ne stire ne rede hym to leue it": 'I will neither advise him to take it for reward, nor persuade him to leave it' [*OED hire* sb. 3. *fig.*]. Ln. "neque tale propositum sibi simpliciter dissuadeo neque suadebo."

211 At the bottom of fol. 6v are the catchwords "in þat."

213 "Fadir of mercy": Cf. 2 Cor. 1:3.

242–43  "schullen more profite finaly to": 'will be ultimately more spir-
itually beneficial to' [*MED profiten* v. 1.(b)]. Ln. "expedient." Cf. "schullen profite to" (Ln. "proficient") in line 220.

270–71  "in testat": 'in evidence' [*OED testate* B. *sb.*, earliest quotation
1619]. Ln. "in statu."

275  "faget": 'a bundle of firewood or kindling' [*MED fagot* n.].

275  In the left margin of fol. 8v is a pointing finger, with "no*ta*"
below.

284  "stillith out": Cf. *OED distil, distill* v. 1. 'to issue forth in drops
or in a fine moisture; to exude.' Ln. "stillat."

295  "for þe hy me*r*cy of Oure Lord God": Cf. Luke 1:78.

301  "sleuthe or lache": Both must be transitive verbs meaning
'lessen' (for Ln. "remittat"), in contrast to "augme*n*te or ecche" (for Ln.
"augeat") at line 303. See *MED sleuthen* v. (b) and *lachen* v. (b) for similar
transitive uses.

312–13  On "þe armes of spiritual kny3thode," see n118 above.

319–20  On the pains of purgatory being more grievous than any pain
on earth, cf. St. Augustine, *Ennarationes in Psalmos,* Ps. 37 (*PL* 36:397):
"Ita plane quamvis salvi per ignem, gravior tamen erit ille ignis, quam
quidquid potest homo pati in hac vita."

320  In the right margin of fol. 10r is "Gregory," with "no*ta*" five
lines below.

320–22  "Seynt Gregori . . . p*ur*gatorie": Following St. Gregory's efficacious prayers for the compassionate and just pagan Trajan, an angel of
God proffers Gregory a choice: "By cause thou hast prayd for a payneme
god graunteth the to chese of ii thynges that one which thou wylt, or thou
schalt be ii dayes in purgatorye in payne, or ellis all the dayes of thy lyf
thou shalt languyssh in sekenesse. Thenne answerd saynt gregory that
he had leuer to haue sekenesse all his lyf in this world, than to fele by ii
dayes the paynes of purgatorye. And euer after he had contynuelly the
feures or axces, or the goute in hys feet . . . ." (Jacobus de Voragine,
*Golden Legend,* 1:414–15). On Jacobus de Voragine's "arithmetic of Pur-

gatory," see Jacques Le Goff, *The Birth of Purgatory,* trans. Arthur Gold-hammer (London: Scolar Press, 1984), 322.

338    In the left margin of fol. 10v are the phrases "*tercia causa*" and "*nota.*"

341–440    "The fyve wyttis of þe body . . . vnclennesse": The discussion of the avoidance of sin moves through a consideration of the Five Bodily Wits. Though not among the rudimentary subjects prescribed by the Council of Lambeth in 1281, the Five Bodily Wits and Five Ghostly Wits were part of the growing list of topics included in the popular religious handbooks of the period. See R. H. Bremmer, *The Fyve Wyttes: A Late Middle English Devotional Treatise Edited from BL MS Harley 2398,* Costerus, n.s., 65 (Amsterdam: Rodopi, 1987), xliii; Harley, "A Fifteenth-Century Manual," 153–54; and *The Lay Folks' Catechism,* ed. T. F. Simmons and H. E. Nolloth, Early English Text Society, o.s., 118 (1901; reprint, Millwood, NY: Kraus, 1973), 19.332–48. The order here—Sight, Hearing, Touch, Smell, and Taste—differs from the order in the later discussion of Christ's suffering in the Five Wits (850–88), where the order is Sight, Hearing, Taste, Smell, and Touch.

349    "sterten here & þere": 'rush, hasten' [*OED start* v. I. 4.a.]. Ln. "vagantibus."

351    "ferue[nt]ne[s]se": There are no attestations in the *MED* or *OED* of the manuscript's "feruenese." Rogers emends to "feruensce," reading the superscript letters as *nc,* but the superscript letters are *ne,* and a subscript carat marks their place between the second *e* and the long *s.* Either *MED fervence* or *ferventnes(se)* will translate Ln. "fervore."

355–56    "wardeyn & keper of þi wyl": Cf. "wardeyn and keper of men" in line 4 above and again in 932 below.

362    "[Dalida]": This error (as well as those in 10 and 38–39) shows the manuscript to be a copy of a Middle English translation.

362–64    "Wheþir . . . strengthe?": See Judg. 16:4–21.

364–66    "Wheþir . . . wyse?": See 3 Kings 11:1–13.

366–68    "Wheþir . . . man-slauȝtre?": See 2 Kings 11:2–27.

368–70    "What . . . þinges?": See Josh. 7:1–26.

370–71   "What . . . tree": See Gen. 2:16–17; 3:1–6.

372–75   "what . . . feendes?": See Judg. 2 and Ezek. 20:14.

378   "þe ere souketh and receyuyth": The translator diverges from the Latin ("auditus suggerit"), describing the ear as a greedy consumer, not merely the messenger or conduit of immoral speech.

379–82   "songes . . . lesynges": Cf. "þe synnes of þe mowthe" in Rolle, "Form of Living," 97.35–98.54.

389   "he openeþ nat þe ʒates": The Middle English translator adds the metaphoric noun to the Latin ("non aperitur").

390   "ys schyt & spered": 'is shut and locked' [*MED speren* v. (1)]. Ln. "obturatur."

395–98   "& naamly . . . wyl": This parenthetical clarification of "recluses" (Ln. "inclusis") is a Middle English addition to the Latin. The Middle English translator, unlike the original author, does not restrict his audience to men; he uses "recluses" broadly to include all religious men and women living in seclusion [*MED reclus(e* n. 1.(b)]. The Middle English translator does not choose the generic term [*MED ancre* n. 1.(a)] or the phrase "ancres & ankeresses" used in line 345, but specifies "anchoresses" as the "more streytly closed" recluses. The use of "ancresse" (Ln. "inclusus") in line 351 is a further instance of the feminine form.

405   In the left margin of fol. 12v is the phrase "no*ta* de luxuria."

405–10   "Alle . . . synne": "All such kinds of lechery are far from a recluse, unless such lechery occurs perchance from a voluptuous delight of the heart in illicit thoughts; and if the thoughts are lingering and are producing a consent to this delight, then without doubt this delight induces a man into deadly sin." Ln. "Ab omnibus huiusmodi luxurie speciebus longe subtrahitur inclusus, nisi forsan a voluptuosa delectacione mentis in ilicita cogitatione, que si morosa fuerit et consensum generans ad sic delectandum, sine dubio peccatum mortale inducit."

406   "ancresse": See 395–98 above.

414   "'molicies'": "[T]he unanimous tradition of the Church through the Reformation, and of Catholicism well into the twentieth century, has been that this word [*mollitia* or *mollicies*] applied to masturba-

tion" (Boswell, *Christianity*, 107). The Middle English text deletes the Latin continuation: "ubi dicit quod 'neque molles, neque masculorum concubitores regnum Dei possidebunt.'"

417   A gap in the line follows the word "temptac*i*on."

419   In the right margin of fol. 13r is the note "narrac*i*o."

423   "ravyssched": The *v* is a supralinear addition.

430–32   On the metaphor of "spirituel bataylle" and spiritual knighthood, see n118 above.

444   "oon": 'only' [*OED one* B.VII.28]. Ln. "solum."

444   In the left margin of fol. 13v is the phrase "no*ta* John Roonling." I find no further record of this name in contemporary records. It is, of course, unclear whether the note identifies one inspired to live an enclosed life or one to whom such inspiration should be an example.

446–47   "as who seyth": On the indefinite relative pronoun *who*, see Tauno F. Mustanoja, *A Middle English Syntax*, Memoires de la Societe Neophilologique de Helsinki, no. 23 (Helsinki: Societe Neophilologique, 1960), 217. Here the phrase translates Latin "quasi," while below at line 496 "As who seyth" translates Latin "ac si diceretur."

453   "entende": See n20 above.

454   "to hys hono*ur* and p[r]esynge": Ln. "eius laudibus."

472   In the lower margin of fol. 14r is a very carelessly drawn circular design that may have originally been intended as a zodiacal chart. No clear connections seem possible, although some of the markings are similar to astrological sigils (see, for example, the sigils in Fred Gettings, *Dictionary of Occult, Hermetic and Alchemical Sigils* [London: Routledge & Kegan Paul, 1981], 315–16).

489   The catchwords "syche in" appear at the bottom of fol. 14v.

496   "As who seyth": See n446–47 above.

508   Without the emendation, which follows the Latin ("in silencio,

in secretis, et in tenebris"), "secret" is ambiguous, either adjective or noun.

516    "oboute": 'about' [*MED aboute(n* adv.].

523    "of": a supralinear addition.

523–24    "lyflode": 'food and drink' [*MED liflod(e* n. 1.(a)]. Ln. "victus."

540    "stronge": The *r* is a supralinear addition.

560    Preceding this line is the title in red ink: "Cap*itul*um p*rimu*m. S*ecun*de p*art*is." The illuminated capital *S* follows.

565–66    "in edificatyf spekynge (*þat* is to sey, in speche strecchinge vn-to v*ertu*)": This is a curious translation of the Latin "in edificatoria leccione," since "reading aloud" would have been more apt than "spekynge" or "speche"; perhaps the translator intends to emphasize oral reading. However, the phrase may be the result of misreading the abbreviated "lectione" as "locutione."

568    "ascendynge or reysynge vp [of] þe herte": Ln. "ascensus mentis." Cf. "þe lyftynge vp of þe herte" (Ln. "elevacio mentis") in line 490. A parallel is found in Hilton's work: "For prayer is nothing other than the ascent of the heart to God, and its withdrawal from all earthly thoughts" (Hilton, *Ladder,* bk. 1, chap. 25, p. 29). Concerning Hilton's definition, Clark and Dorward note that "St. Thomas, following St. John of Damascus, defines prayer as 'an ascent of the mind to God' (*ascensus intellectus in Deum*)," and they consequently observe that "Hilton's approach is more affective" (P. H. Clark and Rosemary Dorward, trans., *The Scale of Perfection,* by Walter Hilton [New York: Paulist Press, 1991], 167 n. 91).

570–71    "nedes . . . required & askyd": 'is necessarily required and asked.' The adverbial genitive "nedes" serves as a modal auxiliary with the past participles "required & askyd." See *MED nedes* adv. (d) for similar uses. Ln. "requiritur."

617    "echyd": 'increased, enhanced, improved' [*MED eken* v. 3.(d).] Ln. "augmentetur."

618    On the primacy of liturgically defined prayer, see Hilton, *Ladder,* bk. 1, chap. 27, pp. 30–31.

625 "Pater Noster": The title is bracketed in red ink and highlighted in yellow.

644 "fe[c]t": This aphetic form of "effect" recurs at line 621. Ln. "effectum."

654–55 "in þe glose of Luk": Ln. "in glossa Luc. 11." The scriptural passage is Luke 11:5–13, Christ's teaching on prayer. The parable of the friend knocking importunately at midnight (vv. 5–8) concludes with the assurance, "Ask, and it shall be given you: seek, and you shall find: knock, and it shall be opened to you. For every one that asketh, receiveth; and he that seeketh, findeth; and to him that knocketh, it shall be opened" (Rheims-Douay Version, vv. 9–10). The gloss may derive from the *Postilla* of Nicholas de Lyra (see Oliger, "Speculum Inclusorum," 87 n. 2).

665 "may speke and trete hys needes": 'may speak and discuss his needs' [*OED treat* v. 2.b.]. Ln. "sua tractare negocia."

667 "medle his speche & his wordis": 'mix his speech and words' [*MED medlen* v. 1.(a)]. Ln. "miscere colloquia."

678 "forȝeu[en]esse": The scribe repeats his error for *MED foryeveness(e* in 681–82 and 952 below.

679 "Petyr . . . God": See Matt. 26:75, Mark 14:72, Luke 22:61–62.

680 "adeuoutrie": 'adultery' [*MED avoutri(e* n.]. Ln. "adulterium."

680–81 "Dauyd . . . manslauȝtre": See 2 Kings 1:13.

681–82 forȝeu[en]esse: See n678 above.

682 "Marie Magdeleyne of hir fornicacion": Just as the conflation of Mary Magdalene with Mary of Bethany resulted in Mary Magdalene's celebrated status as a contemplative (see n34–36 above), the confusion with Mary of Bethany associated Mary Magdalene with sexual sins. Because Mary of Bethany anoints Christ's feet in John 12:1–8 (cf. Matt. 26:6–13), she came to be identified with the unnamed sinful woman who anoints Christ's feet in Luke 7:37–50; a further confusion identifies the sinful woman as the woman taken in adultery (John 8:3–11).

683    "the publican askynge mercy": See Luke 18:13–14.

684–85    "þe people . . . destruccion": See Jon. 3:10.

685–86    "King Dauyd . . . peple": See 2 Kings 24:15–25.

686–88    "Kyng Ezechias . . . lyf": See 4 Kings 20:1–6.

688–91    "and more-ovir . . . God": See 4 Kings 19:35.

690    "C·iiij$^{xx}$·v·m$^l$": '185,000 (or one hundred, four score, and five thousand).' Ln. "centum octoginta quinque millia."

691–94    "Wheþir Moyses . . . preiere?": See Exod. 8 and 17:11–13.

694–98    "Wheþir also Iosue . . . enemys?": See Josh. 10:12–13.

698–703    "Wheþir ek þat Elysee . . . gastnesse?": See 4 Kings 6:18–23 and 7:6–7.

703    "gastnesse": 'fear, terror' [MED gastnes(se n.]. Ln. "terroris."

703–6    "Wheþir eek, by þe preyere of Helye . . . plenteuously?": See 3 Kings 17:1; 18:1, 41–45; Jas. 5:17–18.

706–8    "Wheþir also hertly preyere of Salomon . . . wysdoom?": See 3 Kings 3:6–14.

709–13    "þe preiere of þe hethen kyng, þe gret Alysaundre . . . rebelles": The Latin text continues, "sicut patet in Historia, super librum Hester," referring to the Historia Libri Esther, chapter 5 of the Historia Scholastica of Petrus Comestor (PL 198:1489–1506). For another allusion to Alexander's miracle, see The Metrical Version of Mandeville's Travels, ed. M. C. Seymour, Early English Text Society, o.s., 269 (London: Oxford University Press, 1973), lines 2181–2208.

712–13    "mavmettes": 'pagans, idolaters' [definition unattested for MED maumet n.; cf. MED maumetere n. 'An idolater']. Ln. "ydolatras."

713–16    "þe cursyd & wykkyd kyng Achab . . . hous": See 3 Kings 21:27–29.

746    The initial ȝ is illuminated. At the end of the manuscript line, after "heuynes," is the title "Capitulum Secundum" in red ink.

752–53   "[of] þe greet mercy of his goodnesse": Ln. "ex inmensa misericordia bonitatis."

777   The catchwords "-rie for" appear at the bottom of fol. 22v.

778–84   The discussion of the soul as a trinity ("memorie" or "mynde," "knowynge" or "vndirstond[yng]e," and "loue" or "good wyl"), has its source in Augustine's *memoria, intelligentia,* and *voluntas* or *amor.* See Wolfgang Riehle, *The Middle English Mystics,* trans. Bernard Standring (London: Routledge & Kegan Paul, 1981), 143–44; and Clark and Dorward, *Scale,* 168 n. 108. Cf. lines 1197–1202.

790   The four parts (heart, soul, strength, and mind) are a conflation of the three parts mentioned in each of the two scriptures (Rheims-Douay Version): "Thou shalt love the Lord thy God with thy whole heart, and with thy whole soul, and with thy whole strength" (Deut. 6:5); and "Thou shalt love the Lord thy God with thy whole heart, and with thy whole soul, and with thy whole mind" (Matt. 22:37).

795–97   The Middle English is flawed by homoeoteleuton. Cf. Ln. "ut videlicet omnis operacio anime vel corporis referatur finaliter ad Dei laudem, gloriam et honorem, ut sic omnia fiant finaliter propter amorem Dei."

817–18   "as blyue referre thou & putte al þat": 'may you immediately apply all of that' [*MED blive* adv. 2.; *referren* v. (c)]. Ln. "statim hoc totum referas."

834   In the right margin at the top of fol. 25r is the phrase "nota de passione Xpi."

842–43   "þe Almyȝty Sone of God, þe Kyng of Glorie": Cf. Ln. "Filius Dei, omnipotens rex glorie."

844   In the right margin of fol. 25r is the phrase "nota *contra* desperacionem."

848   "[tri]sty": The scribe erroneously writes "þersty" for Middle English "tristy" [*OED tristy* a.²]. Ln. "tristis." The error may be partially attributable to the scribe's recollection of Christ's words on the cross, "Y thirste" (John 19:28)). In Nicholas Love's early fifteenth-century translation of the pseudo-Bonaventuran *Meditationes Vitae Christi,* Christ's thirst is a topic of extended discussion: "The fifte worde was

*Scicio* / I am athryst. The whiche worde also was occasioun to his moder
and John and other frendes of grete compassioun / and to his wicked
enemyes of grete reioysynge and gladnesse. For þouȝ it so be that it
may be vnderstande that worde *scicio* / I thurste / gostly to that entent
that he threstede aȝeyne the hele of soules; neuerthelesse also in sothen-
esse he thurstede bodely by cause of the grete passynge out of blood /
wher-thoruȝ he was al drye withynneforthe and thursty" (Nicholas Love,
*The Mirrour of the Blessed Lyf of Jesu Christ,* ed. James Hogg and Lawrence F. Powell, Analecta Cartusiana, no. 91 [Salzburg: Institut fur Anglistik und Amerikanistik, 1989], 242).

850–78   "His eyes . . . folkes": See n341–440 above on the Five Bodily Wits.

865   "þo[r]lede & p*er*side": Ln. "perforatum."

866–68   "and his armes and his legges drawen out along w*ith* cordis &
ropes": Such details are similar to the physical description of the Crucifixion in Nicholas Love's *Mirrour of the Blessed Lyf of Jesu Christ:* "And
than he that was on the ladder byhynde the crosse taketh his riȝt hande
and nayleth it faste to the cros: and after he that was on the left side
draweth with all his myȝt the lefte arme and hande and dryueth there-
thorw another grete nayle. . . . Herwith also another harlot renneth to
and draweth downe his feete with all his myȝte; and another anone dryueth a grete longe nayle thoruȝ bothe his feet ioyned to other" (Love,
*Mirrour,* 238–39).

871   "synwes": 'nerves' [*MED sineu* n. 2.]. Ln. "nervi."

875–77   "þe p*re*cious water that stremyd out from his herte, þat was
þerlyd wiþ a scharp spere": See John 19:34. A second allusion occurs at
913–14 (see n913–16 below).

878   "contryt": An erasure of one letter comes between *r* and *y.*

883–84   "þe sonne wyth-drow hys bemes": Cf. Luke 23:45.

885–86   "'The veil . . . erthe'": The emendation corrects the
homoeoteleuton.

900–1   "þe vij*ei* werk*es* of m*er*cy . . . þe vij*ei* deedly synnes": References to the Seven Works of Mercy and the Seven Deadly Sins are com-
monplace in late medieval works of religious instruction, since both topics

were among those prescribed in the canons of the Council of Lambeth in 1281 (*Councils and Synods, with Other Documents Relating to the English Church, Vol. II: A. D. 1205–1313, Part II: 1265–1313,* ed. F. M. Powicke and C. R. Cheney [Oxford: Clarendon Press, 1964], 901, 904–5). See Harley, "A Fifteenth-Century Manual," 151–54; and *Lay Folks' Catechism,* 70.348–62.

901–47   "þe vij^ei deedly synnes . . . werk*es*": The order of the Seven Deadly Sins in this passage—Pride, Envy, Covetousness, Wrath, Gluttony, Lust, and Sloth—differs from the traditional Gregorian order of Pride, Envy, Wrath, Covetousness, Sloth, Gluttony, and Lust. For other examples of Christ's crucifixion as a purgative for the Sins, see Morton W. Bloomfield, *The Seven Deadly Sins: An Introduction to the History of a Religious Concept, with Special Reference to Medieval Literature* (East Lansing: Michigan State College Press, 1952), 167–68, 189, 224, and 229. In the outer margins of fols. 27r and 27v are the notations "ij," "iij," "iiij," "v," and "vj," underlined in red ink and highlighted in yellow.

909   "þe v wyttes": See n341–440 above.

910–11   "þe hu*m*ble & meke inclinac*i*on or bowynge of Cristes heed": See n957–62 below.

913–16   In this passage, the Middle English manuscript lacks the final clause found in the Latin, "quia ipse cecum cor suum perforantem protinus illuminavit." The allusion to Longinus's experience of the healing power of Christ's blood is explained in *The Golden Legend:* "Somme saye that whan he smote our lord wyth spere in the syde, the precious blood aualed by the shafte of the spere vpon hys hondes, and of auenture wyth hys hondes he touched hys eyen, and anon he that had be to fore blynde sawe anon clerly, wherfor he refused all cheualrye and abode wyth thappostles, of whom he was taught and crystened, & after he abandonned to lede an holy lyf in doyng almesses and in kepyng the lyf of a monke about xxxviii yere . . . . (Jacobus de Voragine, *Golden Legend,* 1:416). Additionally, Oliger cites Petrus Comestor, *Historia Scholastica* (*PL* 198:1633). An earlier reference to the spear of Longinus occurs at 875–77 (see n875–77 above).

939–41   "til . . . lecherye": Ln. "donec temptaciones luxurie reprimat in te et evanescat omnis illicita concupiscencia carnis tue."

948   In the right margin of fol. 28r is the phrase, "no*t*a de Helisea proph*e*te."

952    "forȝeu[en]esse": See n678 above.

957–62    "In signe . . . perpetuely": Oliger finds a similar passage in *The
Golden Legend:* "Who is he that is not rauysshid to hope of affyaunce
whiche taketh none hede to the disposicion of his body? he hath his
hede enclyned to be kyssed, the armes stratched tembrace vs, his handes
perced to gyue to vs, the syde open to loue vs, the feet fixed with nayles
for to abyde with vs, and the body stratched all for to gyue to vs" (Jacobus
de Voragine, *Golden Legend,* 1:46). As Riehle succinctly notes, "The
outstretched arms of the crucified saviour were seen as implying the
longing of the suffering lover to receive his beloved, and the gesture of
the bowed head was understood as the wish of God for the kiss of the
soul" (Riehle, *Middle English Mystics,* 39–40). An earlier reference to
Christ's bowed head occurs at lines 910–11. In *The Mirrour of the Blessed
Lyf of Jesu Christ,* the inclination of Christ's head receives a different
interpretation: "And there with he ȝelde the spirite / enclynynge his
heued vppon his brest toward the fader / as in manere of thonkynge that
he cleped hym to hym and ȝeuynge hym his spirite" (Love, *Mirrour,* 243).

962–63    "Ffor vnto the worldys ende, Crist schal duelle with vs
bodyly": Cf. Matt. 28:20.

979–80    "out of þis present ly[ȝt]": Ln. "ab hac luce."

989–90    "sorweful [necessite of þe] departynge of þe soule fro þe
body": Ln. "dolorose separacionis anime a corpore necessitatem."

1005–7    "þe most priue þouȝtes schullen also be cnowe, witnessynge
a mannes owen conscience þat sore fretiþ and gnawyth wyth-ine hym-
self": A second allusion is found in lines 1024–25; and explicit reference
is made later in the chapter (in a passage not found in the defective Middle
English manuscript) to "the immortal worm" ("vermis inmortalis"), an
allusion to Isa. 66:24 or Mark 9:43, 45, 47. On the worm of conscience
as a torment at Judgment, see Marta Powell Harley, "Last Things First
in Chaucer's Physician's Tale: Final Judgment and the Worm of Conscience," *JEGP* 91 (1992): 1–16.

1008–9    "þere schal ben askyd of þe a ful streit acounte of alle þe ȝiftes
þat God hath ȝouen the": The gifts of nature, grace, and fortune serve
as a checklist at Judgment in *The Pricke of Conscience,* ed. Richard
Morris (1863; reprint, New York: AMS Press, 1973), lines 5894–5925.

1024–25    "Wiþ-ineforth þin owen conscience schal sore frete and
gnavve": See n1005–7 above.

1038 "of hem": These catchwords occur at the bottom of fol. 30v.

1044 In the right margin of fol. 31r is the phrase "nota de coronacione Xpi."

1063 "þe serpent of bras . . . temptacion": See Num. 21:6–9.

1064 "smeten": 'smitten, struck' [*MED smiten* v., ppl. *smet(e(n)*].

1091 "may be onyd or knyt to": 'may be mystically united with' [*MED onen* v. (f)]. Ln. "uniatur."

1101 "helpynge": "help" is a later correction, over an erasure.

1103–4 "nat only suffiseth to the he[lth]e of me, but also to al þe worldes helthe": The emendation "helthe" for "herte" follows the Latin ("non solum mihi, sed et toti mundo sufficit ad salutem").

1109 On the metaphor of "spiritual batayle," see n118 above.

1113–14 "al [is] occasion or cause o[f] [m]eede": The emendations in the manuscript's phrase ("al his occasion or cause or neede") follow the Latin ("totum est occasio magni premii").

1131 "of hem þat trauayle": Given the Ln. "itinerancium," the verb must mean 'travel' [*OED travel* 4.a.].

1132 "laboureres": Cf. Ln. "militancium."

1132 "schortly to speke to": 'to be brief' [*MED shortli* adv. 1.(d)]. Ln. "breviter."

1153–66 On Satan's transfiguration as the angel of light, see n174–80 above.

1181–83 "Thus . . . folk'": Ln. "Sic semper servetur vera cordis humilitas, que secundum beatum Augustinum est signum evidentissimum electorum." Oliger rejects the ascription to St. Augustine and cites Gregory the Great's *Moralia in Job* 34.23.56 (*PL* 76:750): " . . . aperte cognoscimus quod evidentissimum reproborum signum superbia est, at contra humilitas electorum."

1184–85  "'God ʒeueth al-only *grace* to hu*m*ble or meke folk*es*'": Cf. Jas. 4:6.

1193  "l[ov]e": Ln. "amorem."

1196  "f[u]lnesse": 'fulness' [*MED fulnes(se* n. Also *volnes(se*]. An unattested spelling for Middle English *fulnesse*, the manuscript's reading "foulnesse" is the familiar spelling of another noun [*MED foulnes(se* n. (a) dirt, filth].

1206–8  "þe Articles of þe Feyth, þat ben conteyned in the Byleve of þe Apostles and in þe Byleve of Athanasie": The fourteen Articles of the Faith are defined in the canons of the Council of Lambeth (*Councils,* 901–2; *Lay Folks' Catechism,* 22.77–30.167). For the Apostles' Creed, see *Lay Folks' Catechism,* 14.223–18.329 and *Documents of the Christian Church,* ed. Henry Bettenson, 2d ed. (Oxford: Oxford University Press, 1963), 23–24. The Athanasian Creed, or *Quicumque,* joins the Apostles' and Nicene Creeds in *The Lay Folks' Catechism:* "Ther be þre credys in þe chirche. / Crede of þe apostelys. *and* Crede of þe chyrche. / and Crede of attanasy. þat was a gret docto*ur*" (14.225–27).

1208  "bele[eu]ed": This emendation of scribal "beleueed" accords with the spelling "beleeuyd" in line 1211.

1215–17  "ffor . . . preef'": Ln. "quia secundum beatum Gregorium, fides non habet meritum, ubi humana ratio prebet experimentum." Oliger cites Gregory the Great's *Homiliae in Evangelia* 2.26.1 (*PL* 76:1197): "nec fides habet meritum, cui humana ratio praebet experimentum." For a quotation of Gregory's passage, see Thomas Aquinas, *De Venerabili Sacramento Altaris,* in *Opuscula Philosophica et Theologica,* ed. A. Michaele de Maria, 3 vols. (Rome, 1996), 3:481.

1236–37  "d[r]eede or wlatsomnesse of a raw body or blood": 'fright, terror' [*MED dred(e* n. 1.(a)]; loathing, disgust' [see *OED wlatsome* a.]. Ln. "ne horror crudi corporis vel sanguinis."

1251  Written up the outer edge of the right margin of fol. 37r is the faint note "a man."

1267–68  "as seith þe philesofr*e* aft*ir* þe oold *tr*anslacion": Ln. "iuxta Philosophum in fine 4 *Methephisicorum* secundum antiquam translacionem." The "oold *tr*anslacion" of Aristotle's *Metaphysics* is apparently either the *Metaphysica Vetustissima,* which contains Books I–IV, 1007a 32–33, or the *Metaphysica Vetus,* which contains one line less than the

*Vetustissima.* However, the passage quoted in the *Speculum Inclusorum* is not found at the end of Book IV of Aristotle's *Metaphysics.* For a thorough outline of the medieval Latin versions of the *Metaphysics,* see James C. Doig, *Aquinas on Metaphysics: A Historico-Doctrinal Study of the "Commentary on the Metaphysics"* (The Hague, Netherlands: Martinus Nijhoff, 1972), 3–10.

1269 "accidentes": 'outward physical characteristics' [*MED accident* n. Pl. *accident(e)s* 2. (a).].

1274–77 "as . . . myrro*ur*": "The breaking of the mirror as a good or bad omen could, of course, involve a feature which was itself conventional: the fact that the fragments of the shattered mirror can still deliver whole images, particularly when these fragments are those of a convex mirror, as they customarily were. This phenomenon was exploited to illustrate the doctrine of transubstantiation: just as the fragments of a broken mirror each furnish a complete image of an object, Christ is wholly present in each fragment of broken bread (the Host); this analogy found almost universal acceptance as a teaching aid in the Middle Ages" (Herbert Grabes, *The Mutable Glass: Mirror-Imagery in Titles and Texts of the Middle Ages and English Renaissance,* trans. Gordon Collier [Cambridge: Cambridge University Press, 1982], 107). See Aquinas, "De Venerabili Sacramento Altaris," 498. For the use of the device in Middle English sermons and homilies, see G. R. Owst, *Literature and Pulpit in Medieval England* (Oxford: Blackwell, 1961), 195. The image is found in the Middle English *Orcherd of Syon,* a fifteenth-century translation of Catherine of Siena's Italian *Dialogue* (completed in 1378): "Riȝt as a myrrour þat is dyuydid, in euery diuysioun is seen þe ymage of a man, and ȝit þe ymage is not diuydid, riȝt so þis hoost [is] diuydid; & ȝit is not diuydid al God and al man, but it is in euery party of it hool and al, ne it is not þerfore lesnyd in itsilf" (Catherine of Siena, *The Orcherd of Syon,* ed. Phyllis Hodgson and Gabriel M. Liegey, Early English Text Society, o.s., 258 [London: Oxford Univ. Press, 1966], 245.34–246.2). In the treatise on the sacrament appended to *The Mirrour of the Blessed Lyf of Jesu Christ,* the image likewise occurs: "Hereto also is a manere likkenesse that we sene in kynde: how the ymage of a mannis grete face and of a grete body is sene in a litel myrour; and if it be broken and departed / ȝit in euery parte hit semeth al the hole ymage / and not in partie after the partes of the glasse so broken" (Love, *Mirrour,* 307).

1280 A spurious addition in red ink occurs at the bottom of fol. 37v, extending the manuscript's customary 23 lines of text to line 25: "which he appeared, is in þe breed and wyn." Cf. Ln. "quo pro nobis passus est in cruce, veraciter est in qualibet hostia consecrata."

# Appendices

## APPENDIX A: LATIN PASSAGES TRANSLATED INTO MODERN ENGLISH

Passages are initially identified by the number of the part, the chapter, and the preceding Middle English line. Parenthetical numbers following each passage refer to the line numbers in Livarius Oliger, "Speculum Inclusorum," *Lateranum,* n.s., 4 (1938): 1–148.

### 1.1.0

"*Videte vocacionem vestram,* o dilectissimi vos inclusi, et ut vos tam operando quam ego exhortando ipsam clarius et efficacius videamus, in principio corditer invocemus auxilium beatissime Trinitatis, Patris et Filii et Spiritus Sancti, qui sunt unus Deus omnipotens, summe sapiens et summe benignus, ut in hoc opere cor meum inspiret, linguam dirigat et manum regulet in scribendo. O dulcissime Domine Ihesu Christe, pro cuius amore solent inclusi perpetuo carceri seipsos voluntarie mancipare, super omnia tuam voluntatem perficere desiderantes, ostendere nun digneris misericorditer mihi nunci tuo . . ." (Oliger 65–66).

### 2.2.1038

". . . contra temptaciones, ad multorum malum exemplum, non iuvisti pacientes in purgatorio per opera caritatis, sed per tuam vitam dampnabilem communem resurreccionis gloriam retardasti, quando etiam celestes orbes, sol, luna cum ceteris planetis et stellis omnibus, terra, mare et elementa singula mutabuntur in septempliciter clariorem seu perfecciorem statum et sic premiabuntur in eterna quiete pro servicio, quod, Deo volente, hominibus temporaliter exhibuerunt. Et ideo hec omnia in circuitu de te, qui suam felicitatem taliter retardasti, modis sibi possibilibus conquerentur. Non igitur sine causa racionabili, si ad iudicium veneris cum mortali peccato, singule creature ad suum iudicem contra te taliter conclamabunt: Vindica, iustissime iudex, non solum tuam iniuriam, sed etiam dampnum illatum tuis omnibus creaturis. Propterea, iuxta consilium prophete David, sepius mentaliter *videte opera Dei terribilis in consiliis super filios hominum.*

"O quam terribilis sentencia, o quam horribilis pena, o quam interminabilis dolor post hunc clamorem sequetur igni eterno iustissime condempnatos. Nam secundum quorumdam Sanctorum sentenciam, in die iudicii omnes sordes, omnes venenosi serpentes et omnes inmundi fetores ad centrum mundi subito descendent, ut ibi tanquam in loco, inferno congruentissimo, sine fine peccatorem puniant. Nec mirum igitur, si infernalis pena sit horribilis et acerba, cum pena purgatorii secundum beatum Augustinum sit *durior quam quicquid penarum videri vel cogitari* poterit *in* hac vita. Torquebunt siquidem sine fine miseros in inferno *ignis inextinguibilis, vermis* inmortalis, sitis insaciabilis, aspectus demonum horribilis, tenebre palpabiles, fetor intolerabilis, de summo frigore in summum calorem subita mutacio, divine visionis et cuiuslibet gaudii carencia, summa cordis tristicia et desperacio cuiuscunque remedii vel succursus. Quia, ut in brevibus multa concludam, nichil erit ibidem delectabile, nulla consolacio, nulla confortacio, sed quodlibet tale erit ibidem quod punire poterit vel nocere, et hoc irremediabiliter sine fine. O igitur anima misera, iuxta consilium prophete Ieremie 2, sepius vide, *quia malum et amarum est reliquisse te Dominum Deum tuum, et non esse timorem* eius *apud te.* Sic conformiter, vos inclusi, per meditacionem tempore necessariam, *videte vocacionem vestram*" (Oliger 100–102).

### 3.1.1038

"Tercio principaliter in hoc opere videbitis, vos inclusi, qualiter exequemini vocacionem vestram. Quia, sicut superius est ostensum, vocati estis ad iugiter orandum, meditandum, legendum vel aliquid honestum manibus operandum. Ideo per consideracionem vestri profectus, vel defectus in istis, videre potestis, qualis fuerit execucio vocacionis vestre.

"Unde primo quo ad oraciones debitas vel consuetas, ad noctem cotidie, priusquam detis oculis vestris sompnum, a vobismet ipsis fidelem compotum mentaliter exigatis: qualiter Dei servicium illo die fuerit persolutum. Si plene, si devote, si sine mentis distraccione, si cum cordis compunccione vel aliquali sanctarum lacrimarum dulcedine solitum pensum solveritis, reddatis Deo gracias cordiales, totum quod bonum est in vestris operibus, sue gracie et misericordie, non vestris virtutibus tribuentes. Si autem diminute, tepide, cum mentis distraccione circa vana, vilia vel inutilia, vel sine devocionis fervore vel dulcedine divinum feceritis servicium, quod omissum est, protinus absolvatur, pro defectus reliquiis pectus tundatur, cordialia suspiria provocentur, pro indulgencia votivis affectibus pulsentur *viscera misericordie Dei nostri,* et vos tali die reputetis fuisse servos malos, *inutiles* et indignos.

"Hic expedit intelligere quam terribiliter sacra Scriptura loquitur de his qui aliquo modo deficiunt in Dei servicio persolvendo. Nam de dicentibus diminute scribitur in Jeremia: *Maledictus qui facit opus* Dei *fraudulenter*. De tepidis in dicendo, qui nec totaliter sunt frigidi per indevocionem et manifestum mortale peccatum, nec ardentes seu calidi per devocionis fervorem, sed quasi accidia et ocio torpentes, dicitur in Apocal.: *Utinam calidus esses aut frigidus, sed quia tepidus es, incipiam te evomere* de *ore meo*. Et de distractis per cogitaciones vanas seu illicitas in orando dicit Dominus indignanter: *Populus* hic *labiis me* honorat, *cor autem* eorum *longe est a me*.

"Contra tales mentis multiplices evagaciones in orando, remedium poterit esse aliquando: si viva voce legatur oracio super librum et interdum de precibus non debitis sed voluntariis, dum in oracione vocali distrahitur quis, statim pro querendo remedio talis oracio sit mentalis. Si neque sic temptator deficiat infestare, queratur ulterius nobilissima medicina . . ." (Oliger 108–109).

3.1.1139

" . . . elemosina Deo . . . , proximis utilissima et fructifera facienti. Sic igitur, vos inclusi, per vestram oracionis examinacionem sollicitam *videte vocacionem vestram*" (Oliger 112–13).

3.2.1139

"Secundo de vestris devotis meditacionibus ad noctem cotidie computetis quantum proficeritis et quantum defeceritis illo die. De quolibet profectu Deo gracias agatis et de quolibet defectu corditer doleatis. Tunc enim proficit meditacio, quando Dei timorem peccatoribus incutit, eius amorem in tepidis et in indevotis accendit, devocionis lacrimas provocat, laudes Dei multiplicat, generat odium peccati et auget desiderium honeste vite atque in celestibus mentem figit. Unde de viro contemplativo dicit propheta quod *sedebit solitarius et tacebit* et levabit se supra *se*. In huiusmodi meditacionibus multi taliter profecerunt, quod aliqualem future beatitudinis dulcedinem pregustabant in delectacione divine bonitatis et eius summe pulcritudinis, in futurorum revelacione, in angelorum collocucione ac etiam in ipsius Omnipotentis aliquali visione et ineffabili consolacione. Iuxta quod dicit propheta David: *Gustate et videte quoniam suavis est Dominus*.

"O gustacio graciosa, o visio preciosa, o suavitas supra cunctas mundi delicias delectabiles. Dum enim solitario contemplanti fervens amor Dei dulcescit, omnis secularis leticia nimirum marcescit. Cui sinamomum sapit et redolet, fex vilis non complacet. Quem amenissimus flos et fructus delectat, deformis stipula non confortat, et cui fons . . ." (Oliger 113–14).

3.2.1280
". . . quo pro nobis passus est in cruce, veraciter est in qualibet hostia consecrata. Nec est hoc Deo difficile qui facit quod eadem vox loquentis multiplicetur naturaliter in singulis auribus auditorum.

"Ulterius adhuc credendum est, quod quelibet parvitas hostie corpus Christi continere poterit, quod prius exivit de clauso Virginis utero et posterius *ianuis clausis* ad discipulos intravit.

"Hic per fidem *state et videte magnalia* Dei, prout Moyses hortabatur populum, Exod. 14. Nam hec omnia firma fide credenda sunt, potissime propter auctoritatem ineffabilis veritatis, que dicit Ioh. 5: *Ego sum panis vite.* Et *si quis manducaverit ex hoc pane, vivet in eternum.* Et *panis quem ego dabo, caro mea est pro mundi vita. Caro mea,* inquit, *vere est cibus et sanguis meus vere est potus.*

"O preciosissimum nutrimentum, o nobilissimum restaurativum, o efficacissimum confortativum, in quo mundis animabus absconditur *omne delectamentum et omnis saporis* suavitas spiritualis! Ad quid queris alibi, o anima misera, solacium, auxilium vel succursum? Alibi sunt creature, hic est Creator omnipotens. Alibi sunt Sanctorum reliquie, hic est omnium Sanctorum conditor, rex et dominus. Nulla alia aliquid facere possunt nisi per virtutem istius. Alia non sunt amanda vel honoranda nisi propter istius amorem, laudem, gloriam et honorem. Hic Deus et Dominus omnium seipsum cotidie liberaliter offert tibi; ut ostendas tuam indigenciam, queras misericordiam, petas graciam et recipias quicquid tibi fuerit necessarium ad salutem. Ne igitur timeas defectum in necessariis, ne paveas in angustiis et tribulacionibus, nec desperes in temptacionibus quibuscunque, quia *Pater* misericordie semper concedet humiliter supplicanti hoc quod petit vel quod melius est petenti.

"His omnibus firmam fidem adhibere debetis, vos inclusi, et sic per sancte meditacionis frequenciam *videte vocacionem vestram*" (Oliger 118–19).

# APPENDIX B: SCRIPTURAL CITATIONS

*Part 1: Index of Scriptural Citations in the Middle English Text*

| *Scripture* | *Line Number(s) in Text* |
|---|---|
| Gen. 1:26 | 776–77 |
| 2:9 | 970 |
| 40:14 | 296 |
| | |
| Deut. 6:5 | 790–91 |
| | |
| 4 Kings 5:10 | 949–50 |
| | |
| Job 7:20 | 4–5 |
| 14:15 | 83–85 |
| | |
| Ps. 18:13 | 1070 |
| 30:13–14 | 384–87 |
| 33:9 | 456 |
| 45:11 | 455–56 |
| 65:5 | 828 |
| 113:9 | 1180–81 |
| 118:37 | 376–77 |
| 144:7 | 1147–49 |
| | |
| Prov. 7:4 | 353–54 |
| 29:23 | 1185–86 |
| | |
| Eccles. 7:29 | 198–99 |
| | |
| Song Sol. 2:7 | 293 |
| 3:5 | 293 |
| 3:11 | 1057–58 |
| | |
| Wisd. 7:13 | 71 |
| 9:15 | 493–95 |
| | |
| Isa. 1:6 | 865–66 |
| 12:3 | 294–95 |
| 29:13 | 480–81 |

| | | |
|---|---|---|
| 1 Cor. | 1:4 | 1178 |
| | 1:14 | 1178 |
| | 1:26 | 159 |
| | 1:28 | 538–40 |
| | 6:10 | 413–14 |
| | 7:20 | 156–58 |
| | 15:10 | 1175 |
| 2 Cor. | 11:14 | 175–76 |
| | 12:2 | 517–19 |
| Eph. | 4:1 | 229–30 |
| 1 Thess. | 4:7 | 448–49 |
| 2 Tim. | 2:3 | 432 |
| | 2:4 | 459 |
| | 2:26 | 63–64 |
| Heb. | 5:7 | 850–51 |
| Jas. | 1:17 | 1176–77 |
| 1 Pet. | 5:5 | 1184–85 |
| 2 John | 1:8 | 121–22 |
| Apoc. | 17:14 | 665–66 |
| | 19:16 | 665–66 |

## Part 2: Scriptural Translation:

Quotations from *The Myrour of Recluses* are identified parenthetically by line number; following each quotation are the two Wycliffite versions printed by Forshall and Madden (W1 and W2 correspond to the left and right columns).

### GENESIS

1:26   "Make we man to þe ymage and oure liknesse" (776–77)
      "Make we man to the ymage and oure lickenesse" (W1)
      "Make we man to oure ymage and liknesse" (W2)

2:9    "[tree of lyf]" (970)
       "tree of lijf" (W1)
       "tre of lijf" (W2)

40:14  "whan it is wiel *with* ʒow, remembrith & þenketh on me"
       (296)
       "haue mynde of me, whanne it were wel with thee" (W1)
       "haue thou mynde on me, whanne it is wel to thee" (W2)

DEUTERONOMY

6:5    "of al þin herte, of al þi soule, of al þi mynde, and of al thi
       *ve*rtu" (790–91)
       "of al thin herte, and of al thi soule, and of alle thi
       strengthis" (W1)
       "of al thin herte, and of al thi soule, and of al thi strengthe"
       (W2)

4 KINGS

5:10   "Wassch þe vij^ei sythes in Iordan, and þi flesch schal receyve
       helþe, and þu schalt be clensyd" (949–50)
       "Goo, and be waschen seuen sithis in Jordan; and thi flesche
       schal receyuen helth, and thou schalt be clensed" (W1)
       "Go thou, and be thou waischun seuensithis in Jordan; and thi
       fleisch shal resseyue helthe, and thou schalt be clensid"
       (W2)

JOB

7:20   "wardeyn and keper of men" (4–5)
       "wardeyn and kep*ere* of men" (1083)
       "kepere of men" (W1)
       "kepere of men" (W2)

14:15  "Thow schalt calle me & I schal ansuere þe. Thow schalt putte
       forth thi ryʒt hand vnto þin handwerk" (83–85)
       "Thou shalt clepe me, and I shal answere to thee; to the werc
       of thin hondis thou shalt putte forth the riʒt hond" (W1)
       "Thou schalt clepe me, and Y schal answere thee; thou schalt

dresse the riȝt half, *that is, blis,* to the werk of thin hon-
dis" (W2)

## PSALMS

18:13  "purge or clense [me] of myn hid synnes" (1070)
"fro myn hid thingis clense me" (W1)
"make thou me cleene fro my priuy synnes" (W2)

30:13–14  "I am maad . . . as a vessel þat ys loost, for I haue herd þe
accusac*i*on or blamynge of many folk þat duellyn in þe circuyt o[r] compas" (384–87)
"I am maad as a vessel lost; for I herde blamyng of manye
duellende in enuyroun" (W1)
"I am maad as a lorun vessel; for Y herde dispisyng of many
men dwellynge in cumpas" (W2)

33:9  "for Oure Lord ys so[o]te and esy" (456)
"for sweete is the Lord" (W1)
"for the Lord is swete" (W2)

45:11  "Taak heede & seeth" (455–56)
"takeþ heede & seeþ" (718)
"Taketh heede, and seeth" (W1)
"ȝyue ȝe tent, and se ȝe" (W2)

65:5  "Seeth þe werk*es* of God" (828)
"seeth the werkis of God" (W1)
"se ȝe the werkis of God" (W2)

113:1  "Lord, nat to vs, nat to vs, but ȝif þow glorie to thi naame"
(1180-81)
"Not to vs, Lord, not to vs; but to thi name ȝif glorie" (W1)
"Lord, not to vs, not to vs; but ȝyue thou glorie to thi
name" (W2)

118:37  "Torne awey myn eyen, lest þei seen or byholde vanyte"
(376–77)
"Turne awei myn eȝen, lest thei see vanytee" (W1)
"Turne thou awei myn iȝen, that tho seen not vanyte" (W2)

144:7  "þey schul telle out or expr*es*se the [mynde of] þe abundaunce
of thi swetnesse" (1147–49)

"The mynde of the abundaunce of thi swetnesse thei shul
 bowen out" (W1)
"Thei schulen bringe forth the mynde of the abundaunce of
 thi swetnesse" (W2)

### PROVERBS

7:4   "[Call] prudence þi love or þi freend" (353–54)
      "prudence clep thou thi lemman" (W1)
      "clepe thou prudence thi frendesse" (W2)

29:23 "and glorie schal exalte or ryse vp hym þat is humble of
      spiryt" (1185–86)
      "and the meke man in spirit glorie shal resceyue" (W1)
      "and glorie schal vp take a meke man of spirit" (W2)

### ECCLESIASTES

7:29  "I foond . . . o man among a M¹" (198–99)
      "A man of a thousend oon I fond" (W1)
      "I foon o man of a thousynde" (W2)

### SONG OF SOLOMON

2:7   "I preie & biseche ȝow" (293)
      "I adiure ȝou" (W1)
      "Y charge ȝou greetli" (W2)

3:5   "I preie & biseche ȝow" (293)
      "I adiure ȝou" (W1)
      "Y charge yow greetli" (W2)

3:11  "Seeth þe Kyng Salomon wyth þe dyademe wiþ þe which his
      modir coronyd hym" (1057–58)
      "seeth . . . king Salamon in the diademe, in the whiche
      crounede hym hys moder" (W1)
      "se kyng Salomon in the diademe, bi which his modir
      crownede hym" (W2)

### WISDOM

7:13  "wiþ-oute feynynge" (71)
      "withoute feynyng" (W1)

"with out feynyng" (W2)

9:15   "The body þat is corrupt greuyt[h] þe soule, and an erthely
        inhabitacion þrestith dovn þe wyt, þenkynge many þin-
        ges" (493–95)
        "the body that is corumpid, greeueth the soule; and ertheli
        indwelling presseth doun the wit, manye thingus then-
        kende" (W1)
        "the bodi that is corrupt, greueth the soule; and ertheli
        dwellyng pressith doun the wit, thenkynge many thingis"
        (W2)

ISAIAH

1:6    "fro þe sole of þe foot vn-to þe top of his heed" (865–66)
        "Fro the plante of the foot vnto the top" (W1)
        "Fro the sole of the foot til to the nol" (W2)

12:3   "drawen watres in ioye of þe welles of Oure Saueour" (294–95)
        "ȝee shul drawe watris in ioȝe of the welles of the saueour"
        (W1)
        "ȝe schulen drawe watris with ioie of the wellis of the sauy-
        our" (W2)

29:13  "This peple worschepyth me wiþ her tonges, but her herte ys
        fer fro me" (480–81)
        "this puple neȝheth with his mouth, and with his lippes glori-
        fieth me, his herte forsothe fer is fro me" (W1)
        "this puple neiȝeth with her mouth, and glorifieth me with
        her lippis, but her herte is fer fro me" (W2)

JEREMIAH

17:14  "Hele me, Lord, and I schal ben helyd; make me saaf and I
        schal be sauyd" (1071–72)
        "Hele me, Lord, and Y shal ben helid; saf mac me and Y shal
        be saf" (W1)
        "Lord, heele thou me, and Y schal be heelid; make thou me
        saaf, and Y schal be saaf" (W2)

LAMENTATIONS

1:12   "Taketh hede . . . and seeth ȝif þer be any sorwe lyk to my
        sorwe" (892–93)
        "taketh heed, and seeth, if ther is sorewe as my sorewe" (W1)
        "perseyue, and se, if ony sorewe is as my sorewe" (W2)

MALACHI

1:11 "a clene oblac*i*on & offrynge" (1138)
"a cleene offryng" (W1)
"a cleene offring" (W2)

2 MACCABEES

12:46 "Therfor, yt is ful holy and hoo[l]su*m* to p*r*eye for hem þat
ben deede, þat þey may ben dissoluyd and vnknet of her
synnes" (324–26)
"Therfore holy and helthful thenkynge is, for to preye for dead
men, that thei be vnbounden fro synnus" (W1)
"Therfor hooli and heelful thenkyng is, for to preie for deed
men, that thei be releesid of synnes" (W2)

MATTHEW

5:12 "beth ioyful and gladiþ" (271)
"Ioye ȝee with yn forth, and glade ȝee with out forth" (W1)
"Ioie ȝe, and be ȝe glad" (W2)

12:36 "ydyl word" (995)
"ydel word" (W1)
"idel word" (W2)

15:8 "This peple worschepyth me wiþ her tonges, but her herte ys
fer fro me" (480–81)
"This peple honoureth me with lippis, forsothe her herte is
fer fro me" (W1)
"This puple honourith me with lippis, but her herte is fer fro
me" (W2)

20:16 "Many ben callyd & fewe ben chosen" (263–64)
"many ben clepid, bot few chosun" (W1)
"many ben clepid, but fewe *ben* chosun" (W2)

22:37 "of al þin herte, of al þi soule, of al þi mynde, and of al thi
ve*r*tu" (790–91)
"of al thin herte, and in al thi soule, and in al thi mynde" (W1)
"of al thin herte, and in al thi soule, and in al thi mynde" (W2)

22:38 "þe firste & grettest co*m*maundement" (789)

"the firste and the most maundement" (W1)
"the firste and the moste maundement" (W2)

24:13    "schul p*erseuere* and contynue vn-to þe ende" (334–35)
         "schal dwelle stable vnto the ende" (W1)
         "schal dwelle stable in to the ende" (W2)

26:38    Ffor his "soule" was "[tristy] vn-to þe deeþ" (848)
         "My soule is sorowful til to the deth" (W1)
         "My soule is soreuful to the deeth" (W2)

27:45    "& derknesses apperden on the erthe" (884)
         "dercnessis ben maad on al the erthe" (W1)
         "derknessis weren maad on al the erthe" (W2)

27:51–52  "[The veil of the temple was torn atwo; the erthe] quok; the
         dede man roos vp; and the harde stones . . . weren kut
         atwo" (885–90)
         "the veile of the temple is kitt, *or rent,* in to two parties . . . .
         And the erthe is moued, and stoonys ben cleft; and biriels
         ben openyd" (W1)
         "the veil of the temple was to-rent in twey parties . . . . And
         the erthe schoke, and stoonus were cloue; and birielis weren
         openyd" (W2)

### MARK

7:6      "This peple worschepyth me wiþ her tonges, but her herte ys
         fer fro me" (480–81)
         "This peple worschipith me with lippis, forsothe her herte is
         fer fro me" (W1)
         "This puple worschipith me with lippis, but her herte is fer
         fro me" (W2)

11:24    "Alle þinges þat ȝe þat p*reien asken, byleueth þat ȝe schullen
         haue hem, & þei schullen falle vn-to ȝow" (651–53)
         "alle thingis what euere thingis ȝe preiynge schulen axe,
         bileue ȝe that ȝe schulen take, and thei schulen come to
         ȝou" (W1)
         "alle thingis what euer thingis ȝe preynge schulen axe, bileue
         ȝe that ȝe schulen take, and thei schulen come to ȝou"
         (W2)

13:33    "Seeth, waketh, and pᵣeyeth" (610)
        "Se ʒe, wake ʒe, and preie ʒe" (W1)
        "Se ʒe, wake ʒe, and preie ʒe" (W2)

14:34    Ffor his "soule" was "[tristy] vn-to þe deeþ" (848)
        "My soule is sorwful til to the deeth" (W1)
        "My soule is soreweful to the deeth" (W2)

## LUKE

2:14    "Glorie & ioye be to God on hy" (1179)
        "Glorie *be* in the hiʒeste thingis to God" (W1)
        "Glorie *be* in the hiʒeste thingis to God" (W2)

5:32    "I cam nat to penaunce to calle ry[ʒt]wys folk, but synneres"
        (166-67)
        "I cam not to clepe iust men, but synful men to penaunce"
        (W1)
        "Y cam not to clepe iuste men, but synful men to pen-
        aunce" (W2)

10:20    "þat ʒoure names bien wretyn in heuene" (273)
        "that ʒoure names ben writun in heuenes" (W1)
        "that ʒoure names ben writun in heuenes" (W2)

10:42    Marie Maudeleyne, which "chees þe beste paart" (35–36)
        "Marie hath chose the beste part" (W1)
        "Marie hath chosun the best part" (W2)

22:44    "þe dropes of þe blody swoot of Crist þat fil doun to þe er-
        the" (930–31)
        "his swoot was maad as dropis of blood rennynge doun in to
        the erthe" (W1)
        "his swot was maad as dropis of blood rennynge doun in to
        the erthe" (W2)

23:44    "& derknesses apperden on the erthe" (884)
        "and derknessis weren maad in al erthe" (W1)
        "and derknessis weren maad in al the erthe" (W2)

23:45    "[The veil of the temple was torn atwo]" (885–86)
        "the veyl of the temple was kitt the myddel" (W1)
        "the veile of the temple was to-rent atwo" (W2)

23:48   "cnokkydon her brest*es*" (882)
        "smytinge her brestis" (W1)
        "smyten her brestis" (W2)

24:38–39   "Whi or wher-to be ȝe troublyd, and whi ascenden þouȝtes
           in-to ȝoure hertes? Byholdeth myn handes and my feet"
           (1059–61)
           "What ben ȝe troublid, and thouȝtis styȝen vp in to ȝoure
           hertis? Se ȝe myn hondis and my feet" (W1)
           "What ben ȝe troblid, and thouȝtis comen vp in to ȝoure
           hertis? Se ȝe my hoondis and my feet" (W2)

JOHN

9:7     Who schal "wassche" my felþes "wiþ þe watres of Syloe"
        (291)
        "Go, and be thou wayschen in the watir, *or cisterne,* of
        Siloe" (W1)
        "Go, and be thou waisschun in the watir of Siloe" (W2)

9:11    Who schal "wassche" my felþes "wiþ þe watres of Syloe"
        (291)
        "Go thou to the watir, *or cisterne,* of Siloe, and waische" (W1)
        "Go thou to the watre of Siloe, and wassche" (W2)

ROMANS

1:30    "hatful to God" (404)
        "hateful to God" (W1)
        "hateful to God" (W2)

8:28    "To hem þat loven God, alle þing*es* werkyn in-to good or wer-
        kyn wiel and taken good effect, to hem þat aftir hir *p*urpos
        bien callid seyntes" (254–56)
        "for to men louynge God alle thingis worchen to gidere into
        good thing, to hem that aftir purpos ben clepid seyntis"
        (W1)
        "to men that louen God, alle thingis worchen togidere in to
        good, to hem that aftir purpos ben clepid seyntis" (W2)

8:30    "tho that God hath *p*redestyned, he hath callyd hem so; and
        wham he clepte in þat man*er*e, hem, ȝif þat þ[ei] falle, he
        iustifieth bi grace of penaunce; and wham þat he iustifieþ

so, hem he magnifieþ be habundaunce and plente of *grac*e
and *ve*rtu" (264–68)

"whom he bifore ordeynede to blisse, and hem he clepide; and
whom he clepide, and hem he iustifiede; sothli whom he
iustifiede, and hem he glorifiede" (W1)

"thilke that he bifore ordeynede to blis, hem he clepide; and
whiche he clepide, hem he iustifiede; and whiche he iustifiede, and hem he glorifiede" (W2)

9:12　"nat of þe meryt or meede of a man or of his werk*es,* but of
God þat calliþ hym" (550–51)
"not of workis, but of *God* clepinge" (W1)
"not of werkis, but of God clepynge" (W2)

11:33　"O þe heyȝnesse of þe wysdom and science of God" (245)
"A! the hiȝnesse, *or depnesse,* of the richesse of wysdom and
kunnynge of God" (W1)
"O! the heiȝnesse of the ritchessis of the wisdom and of the
kunnyng of God" (W2)

13:10　"The foulnesse or abundaunce of lawe ys loue" (1196–97)
"loue is the plente, *or fulfillinge,* of the lawe" (W1)
"loue is the fulfillyng of the lawe" (W2)

## I CORINTHIANS

1:4　"I ȝelde þonkynges to God" (1178)
"I do thankyngis to my God" (W1)
"Y do thankyngis to my God" (W2)

1:14　"I ȝelde þonkynges to God" (1178)
"I do thankyngis to God" (W1)
"Y do thankyngis to my God" (W2)

1:26　"seeth now ȝour*e* callynge and clepynge" (159)
"seeþ ȝoure clepynge and callynge" (337)
"seeþ so ȝoure clepynge" (450)
"byholdeþ & seeþ ȝour*e* callynge" (559)
"by-holdeþ and seeþ [3]our*e* callynge" (745)
"se ȝe ȝour*e* clepinge" (W1)
"se ȝe ȝoure clepyng" (W2)

1:28　"God calleþ "þo þinges þat ben nat" as "tho þinges þat ben,"

"and þe seke & þe feeble þinges of þe world haþ God chosen
for to confunde & scheende alle stronge þinges" (538–40)

"and God chees the syke thingis, *or freel,* of the world, that
he confounde the stronge thingis; and God chees . . . tho
thingis that ben not, that he schulde distroye tho thingis that
ben" (W1)

"and God chees the feble thingis of the world, to confounde
the stronge thingis; and God chees . . . tho thingis that ben
not, to distruye tho thingis that ben" (W2)

6:10  "lecherie agayn kynde," "'molicies'" (413–14)
"neische" (W1)
"letchouris aȝen kynde" (W2)

7:20  "Lat eu*er*y man duuelle to-ward God in þe same callynge þat
he ys clepyd" (156–58)
"in þe clepynge which ȝe ben clept vnto" (335–36)
"Ech man in what clepyng he is clepid, in that dwelle he" (W1)
"Ech man in what clepyng he is clepid, in that dwelle he" (W2)

15:10  "By the gr*a*ce of God, I am þat I am" (1175)
"by the grace of God, I am that thing that I am" (W1)
"bi the grace of God Y am that thing that Y am" (W2)

## 2 CORINTHIANS

11:14  "þe angel Sathenas, þat ofte-tymes t*r*ansfigureth hym in-to þe
aungel of lyȝt" (175–76)
"the angel of Sathenas, *t*ransfygurynge hym in-to þe angel of
lyȝt" (1154–55)
"he Sathanas transfygurith him into an aungel of lyȝt" (W1)
"Sathanas hym silf transfigurith hym in to an aungel of
light" (W2)

12:2  "As Seynt Pouel, þat was "rauysschid in-to þe þrydde
heuene," he wyste nat wheþir he was "wi*th*-ine his body"
or "wi*th*-oute his body" (517–19)
"wher in body, wher out of body, I woot not, God woot; sich
a man rauyschid til to the thridde heuene" (W1)
"whether in bodi, whether out of the bodi, Y woot not, God

woot; that siche a man was rauyschid til to the thridde heuene" (W2)

**EPHESIANS**

4:1 "I byseche ȝow þat ȝe walke & go worthili in þe callinge in which ȝe ben cleept" (229–30)
"I . . . byseche, that ȝe walke worthily in the clepinge, in which ȝe ben clepid" (W1)
"Y . . . biseche ȝou, that ȝe walke worthili in the clepyng, in which ȝe ben clepid" (W2)

**I THESSALONIANS**

4:7 "God callyd vs nat in-to clennesse, but in-to satisfaccion" (448–49)
"God clepide not vs into vnclennesse, but into hoolynesse" (W1)
"God clepide not vs in to vnclennesse, but in to holynesse" (W2)

**2 TIMOTHY**

2:3 "Cristes knyth" (432)
"a good knyȝt of Crist Jhesu" (W1)
"a good knyȝt of Crist Jhesu" (W2)

2:4 "medlen wiþ worldly needes" (459)
"inwlappith him silf with worldli nedis" (W1)
"wlappith hym silf with worldli nedis" (W2)

2:26 "þe feendes snares" (63–64)
"snaris of the deuyl" (W1)
"the snares of the deuel" (W2)

**HEBREWS**

5:7 "bitter teres with a loud & greet cry" (850–51)
"with greet cry and teeris" (W1)
"with greet cry and teeris" (W2)

**JAMES**

1:17 "euery good ȝefte & euery perfyt ȝefte from above ys de-scendynge from þe Fadir of lyȝt" (1176–77)

"Ech best thing ȝouun, and al parfijt ȝift is fro aboue, comynge doun of the fadir of liȝtis" (W1)

"Ech good ȝifte, and ech perfit ȝifte is from aboue, and cometh doun fro the fadir of liȝtis" (W2)

## I PETER

5:5    "God ȝeueth al-only *grace* to hum̃ble or meke folk*es*"
(1184–85)

"he ȝiueth grace to meke men" (W1)

"he ȝyueth grace to meke men" (W2)

## 2 JOHN

1:8    "Seeth and beholdiþ ȝoure owen self, lest ȝe lese þat þat ȝe
haan doon and wrouȝt" (121–22)

"See ȝe ȝoure silf, lest ȝe leese the thinges that ȝe han
wrought" (W1)

"Se ȝe ȝou silf, lest ȝe lesen the thingis that ȝe han
wrouȝt" (W2)

## APOCALYPSE

17:14    "þe Kyng of alle kynges" (665–66)

"kyng of kyngis" (W1)

"kyng of kyngis" (W2)

19:16    "þe Kyng of alle kynges" (665–66)

"Kyng of kyngis" (W1)

"Kyng of kyngis" (W2)

# APPENDIX C: INDEX OF NAMES

In this alphabetical list of the names found in the Middle English text, each entry records the first spelling and all line numbers; titles or honorifics (e.g., "King," "þe prophete," "Seynt") are deleted. The common references to the Trinity are not indexed.

# Works Cited

Ackerman, Robert W., and Roger Dahood, eds. and trans. *Ancrene Riwle: Introduction and Part I.* Medieval and Renaissance Texts and Studies, no. 31. Binghamton, NY: Center for Medieval and Early Renaissance Studies, 1984.

Aelred of Rievaulx. *Aelred of Rievaulx's "De Institutione Inclusarum": Two English Versions.* Edited by John Ayto and Alexandra Barratt. Early English Text Society, o.s., 287. New York: Oxford University Press, 1984.

Aquinas, Thomas. "De Venerabili Sacramento Altaris." In *Opuscula Philosophica et Theologica,* edited by A. Michaele de Maria. 3 vols. Rome, 1886.

Benedictine Monks of St. Augustine's Abbey, comps. *The Book of Saints: A Dictionary of Servants of God Canonized by the Catholic Church.* 6th ed. London: A & C Black, 1989.

Blake, Norman F. "Varieties of Middle English Religious Prose." In *Chaucer and Middle English Studies in Honour of Rossell Hope Robbins,* edited by Beryl Rowland, 348–56. London: George Allen & Unwin, 1974.

Bloomfield, Morton W. *The Seven Deadly Sins: An Introduction to the History of a Religious Concept, with Special Reference to Medieval Literature.* East Lansing: Michigan State College Press, 1952.

Boswell, John. *Christianity, Social Tolerance, and Homosexuality: Gay People in Western Europe from the Beginning of the Christian Era to the Fourteenth Century.* Chicago: University of Chicago Press, 1980.

Bowker, Margaret. *The Secular Clergy in the Diocese of Lincoln, 1495–1520.* Cambridge Studies in Medieval Life and Thought, n.s., 13. Cambridge: Cambridge University Press, 1968.

Bremmer, R. H. *The Fyve Wyttes: A Late Middle English Devotional Treatise Edited from BL MS Harley 2398.* Costerus ns 65. Amsterdam: Rodopi, 1987.

*Calendar of the Patent Rolls, Preserved in the Public Record Office: Edward IV, Edward V, Richard III, A.D. 1476–1485.* London: Mackie, for His Majesty's Stationery Office, 1901.

*Calendar of the Patent Rolls, Preserved in the Public Record Office: Henry VII, Volume I, A.D. 1485–1494.* London: Hereford Times, for His Majesty's Stationery Office, 1914.

Catherine of Siena. *The Orcherd of Syon.* Edited by Phyllis Hodgson and Gabriel M. Liegey. Early English Text Society, o.s., 258. London: Oxford University Press, 1966.

*The Catholic Encyclopedia.* 1907 ed.

Chaucer, Geoffrey. *The Riverside Chaucer.* Edited by Larry D. Benson. þd ed. Boston: Houghton Mifflin, 1987.

Clay, Rotha Mary. *The Hermits and Anchorites of England.* 1914. Reprint. Detroit: Singing Tree Press, 1968.

————. *The Mediaeval Hospitals of England.* 1909. Reprint. London: Frank Cass, 1966.

Clark, P. H., and Rosemary Dorward, trans. *The Scale of Perfection,* by Walter Hilton. New York: Paulist Press, 1991.

Colledge, Eric, ed. *The Mediaeval Mystics of England.* New York: Charles Scribner's Sons, 1961.

*Councils and Synods, with Other Documents Relating to the English Church, Vol. II: A. D. 1205–1313, Part II: 1265–1313.* Edited by F. M. Powicke and C. R. Cheney. Oxford: Clarendon Press, 1964.

D'Evelyn, Charlotte. "Instructions for Religious." In *A Manual of the Writings in Middle English, II,* edited by J. Burke Severs, 458–81, 650–59. Hamden: Connecticut Academy of Arts and Sciences, 1970.

*Documents of the Christian Church.* Edited by Henry Bettenson. 2d ed. Oxford: Oxford University Press, 1963.

Doig, James C. *Aquinas on Metaphysics: A Historico-Doctrinal Study of the Commentary on the Metaphysics.* The Hague, Netherlands: Martinus Nijhoff, 1972.

*The Early South-English Legendary.* Edited by Carl Horstmann. Early English Text Society, o.s., 87. 1887. Reprint. Millwood, NY: Kraus, 1973.

Ellis, R. "The Choices of the Translator in the Late Middle English Period." In *The Medieval Mystical Tradition in England: Papers Read at Dartington Hall, July 1982,* edited by Marion Glasscoe, 18–46. Exeter: University of Exeter, 1982.

Emden, A. B. *A Biographical Register of the University of Cambridge.* Cambridge, 1963.

————. *A Biographical Register of the University of Oxford to A.D. 1500.* 3 vols. Oxford, 1957–59.

Evans, Michael. "An Illustrated Fragment of Peraldus's *Summa* of Vice: Harleian MS 3244." *Journal of the Warburg and Courtauld Institutes* 45 (1982): 14–68.

Foot, Mirjam. Letter to author, 25 June 1990.

Foster, C. W., and A. H. Thompson, eds. "The Chantry Certificates for Lincoln and Lincolnshire, Returned in 1548." *Associated Architectural Societies' Reports and Papers* 37.1–2 (1923–26): 100–106, 250–51 (nos. 115–23).

Gettings, Fred. *Dictionary of Occult, Hermetic and Alchemical Sigils.* London: Routledge & Kegan Paul, 1981.

Grabes, Herbert. *The Mutable Glass: Mirror-Imagery in Titles and Texts of the Middle Ages and English Renaissance.* Translated by Gordon Collier. Cambridge: Cambridge University Press, 1982.

Harley, Marta Powell. "A Fifteenth-Century Manual of Religious Instruction in Bodleian Library MS. Tanner 201." *Fifteenth-Century Studies* 15 (1989): 147–64.

————. "Last Things First in Chaucer's Physician's Tale: Final Judgment and the Worm of Conscience." *JEGP* 91 (1992): 1–16.

————. *A Revelation of Purgatory by an Unknown, Fifteenth-Century Woman Visionary: Introduction, Critical Text, and Translation.* Studies in Women and Religion 18. New York: Edwin Mellen Press, 1985.

Hilton, Walter. *The Ladder of Perfection*. Translated by Leo Sherley-Price. 1957. Reprint. New York: Penguin, 1988.

Hodgson, Phyllis. *"The Cloud of Unknowing" and Related Treatises*. Analecta Cartusiana, no. 3. Salzburg: Institut für Anglistik und Amerikanistik, 1982.

*The Holy Bible Made from the Latin Vulgate by John Wycliffe and His Followers*. Edited by Josiah Forshall and Frederic Madden. 1850. Reprint. New York: AMS Press, 1982.

*The Holy Bible Translated from the Latin Vulgate: Douay-Rheims Version*. Rev. Bishop Richard Challoner. 1749–52. Rockford, IL: TAN Books, 1989.

Hussey, S. S. "The Audience for the Middle English Mystics." In *De Cella in Seculum: Religious and Secular Life and Devotion in Late Medieval England*, edited by Michael G. Sargent, 109–22. Cambridge: D. S. Brewer, 1989.

Jacobus de Voragine. *The Golden Legend of Master William Caxton Done Anew*. 3 vols. London, 1892.

Jolliffe, P. S. *A Check-List of Middle English Prose Writings of Spiritual Guidance*. Toronto: Pontifical Institute of Mediaeval Studies, 1974.

Keiser, George R. "'Noght how lang man lifs; bot how wele': The Laity and the Ladder of Perfection." In *De Cella in Seculum: Religious and Secular Life and Devotion in Late Medieval England*, edited by Michael G. Sargent, 145–59. Cambridge: D. S. Brewer, 1989.

Knowles, David. *The Religious Orders in England, Volume II: The End of the Middle Ages*. Cambridge: Cambridge University Press, 1955.

Knowles, David, and R. Neville Hadcock. *Medieval Religious Houses: England and Wales*. 1953. London: Longmans, Green, 1971.

Lagorio, Valerie M. "Problems in Middle English Mystical Prose." In *Middle English Prose: Essays on Bibliographical Problems*, edited by A. S. G. Edwards and Derek Pearsall, 123–48. New York: Garland, 1981.

*The Lay Folks' Catechism*. Edited by T. F. Simmons and H. E. Nolloth. Early English Text Society, o.s., 118. 1901. Reprint. Millwood, NY: Kraus, 1973.

Le Goff, Jacques. *The Birth of Purgatory*. Translated by Arthur Goldhammer. London: Scolar Press, 1984.

Leland, John. *The Itinerary of John Leland, in or about the Years 1535–1543*. Edited by Lucy Toulmin Smith. 5 vols. 1907. Reprint. London: Centaur, 1964.

Le Neve, John. *Fasti Ecclesiae Anglicanae, 1300–1541: I. Lincoln Diocese*. Compiled by H. P. F. King. London: Athlone Press, 1962.

*Lincoln Wills, 1271–1530*. 2 vols. Lincoln Record Society, no. 5 (1914) and no. 10 (1918).

Love, Nicholas. *The Mirrour of the Blessed Lyf of Jesu Christ*. Edited by James Hogg and Lawrence F. Powell. Analecta Cartusiana, no. 91. Salzburg: Institut für Anglistik und Amerikanistik, 1989.

McIntosh, Angus, M. L. Samuels, and Michael Benskin. *A Linguistic Atlas of Late Medieval English*. 4 vols. Aberdeen: Aberdeen University Press, 1986.

*The Metrical Version of Mandeville's Travels*. Edited by M. C. Seymour. Early English Text Society, o.s., 269. London: Oxford University Press, 1973.

*Middle English Dictionary*. 1954–.

Milosh, Joseph E. "*The Scale of Perfection* and the Religious-Handbook Tradition." In *"The Scale of Perfection" and the English Mystical Tradition*, 140–68. Madison: University of Wisconsin Press, 1966.

Mustanoja, Tauno F. *A Middle English Syntax*. Memoires de la Societe Neophilologique de Helsinki, no. 23. Helsinki: Societe Neophilologique, 1960.

Oliger, Livarius. "Speculum Inclusorum." *Lateranum*, n.s., 4 (1938): 1–148.

Owst, G. R. *Literature and Pulpit in Medieval England*. Oxford: Blackwell, 1961.

*Oxford English Dictionary*. 2d ed. 1989.

Parkes, Malcolm B. Letter to author, 20 June 1990.

*Patrologiae Cursus Completus. Series Latina (PL)*. Edited by J.-P. Migne. 221 vols. Paris, 1844–1903.

Peck, Francis. *Academia Tertia Anglicana or The Antiquarian Annals of Stanford*. 1727. Reprint. East Ardsley, Eng.: EP Publishing, 1979.

*The Pricke of Conscience*. Edited by Richard Morris. 1863. Reprint. New York: AMS Press, 1973.

Riehle, Wolfgang. *The Middle English Mystics*. Translated by Bernard Standring. London: Routledge & Kegan Paul, 1981.

Rogers, Lillian E. "Edition of British Museum MS. Harley 2372 (Advice to Recluses)." B. Litt. thesis, Oxford University, 1933.

Rolle, Richard. "The Form of Living." In *English Writings of Richard Rolle, Hermit of Hampole*, edited by Hope Emily Allen, 82–118. 1931. Reprint. Gloucester, Eng.: Sutton, 1988.

Salu, M. B., trans. *The Ancrene Riwle (The Corpus MS.: Ancrene Wisse)*. Notre Dame, IN: University of Notre Dame Press, 1956.

*The South English Legendary, Volume 1*. Edited by C. D'Evelyn and A. J. Mill. Early English Text Society, o.s., 235. London: Oxford University Press, 1959.

*Victoria County History, Lincolnshire*. Vol. 2.

Warren, Ann K. "Old Forms with New Meanings: Changing Perceptions of Medieval English Anchorites." *Fifteenth-Century Studies* 5 (1982): 209–21.

Wright, Cyril Ernest, and Ruth C. Wright, eds. *The Diary of Humfrey Wanley, 1715–1726*. 2 vols. London: Bibliographical Society, 1966.